PRENTICE HALL

SCIENCE EXPLORER

Chemical Building Blocks

PRENTICE HALL
Needham, Massachusetts
Upper Saddle River, New Jersey

Chemical Building Blocks

Program Resources

Student Edition
Annotated Teacher's Edition
Teaching Resources Book with Color Transparencies
Chemical Building Blocks Materials Kits

Program Components

Integrated Science Laboratory Manual
Integrated Science Laboratory Manual, Teacher's Edition
Inquiry Skills Activity Book
Student-Centered Science Activity Books
Program Planning Guide
Guided Reading English Audiotapes
Guided Reading Spanish Audiotapes and Summaries
Product Testing Activities by Consumer Reports™
Event-Based Science Series (NSF funded)
Prentice Hall Interdisciplinary Explorations
Cobblestone, Odyssey, Calliope, and *Faces* Magazines

Media/Technology

Science Explorer Interactive Student Tutorial CD-ROMs
Odyssey of Discovery CD-ROMs
Resource Pro® (Teaching Resources on CD-ROM)
Assessment Resources CD-ROM with Dial-A-Test®
Internet site at www.science-explorer.phschool.com
Life, Earth, and Physical Science Videodiscs
Life, Earth, and Physical Science Videotapes

Science Explorer Student Editions

From Bacteria to Plants

Animals

Cells and Heredity

Human Biology and Health

Environmental Science

Inside Earth

Earth's Changing Surface

Earth's Waters

Weather and Climate

Astronomy

Chemical Building Blocks

Chemical Interactions

Motion, Forces, and Energy

Electricity and Magnetism

Sound and Light

Staff Credits

The people who made up the *Science Explorer* team—representing editorial, editorial services, design services, field marketing, market research, marketing services, on-line services/multimedia development, product marketing, production services, and publishing processes—are listed below. Bold type denotes core team members.

Kristen E. Ball, **Barbara A. Bertell,** Peter W. Brooks, **Christopher R. Brown, Greg Cantone,** Jonathan Cheney, **Patrick Finbarr Connolly,** Loree Franz, Donald P. Gagnon, Jr., **Paul J. Gagnon, Joel Gendler,** Elizabeth Good, Kerri Hoar, **Linda D. Johnson,** Katherine M. Kotik, Russ Lappa, Marilyn Leitao, David Lippman, **Eve Melnechuk, Natania Mlawer,** Paul W. Murphy, **Cindy A. Noftle,** Julia F. Osborne, Caroline M. Power, Suzanne J. Schineller, **Susan W. Tafler,** Kira Thaler-Marbit, Robin L. Santel, Ronald Schachter, **Mark Tricca,** Diane Walsh, Pearl B. Weinstein, Beth Norman Winickoff

Acknowledgment for page 143: Excerpt from *The Iron Peacock* by Mary Stetson Clarke. Copyright ©1966 by Mary Stetson Clarke. Published by Viking Press.

ISBN 0-13-434480-4

 6 7 8 9 10   03 02 01 00

Cover: These crystals are made of sulfur, one of the many elements that are the building blocks of matter.

Program Authors

Michael J. Padilla, Ph.D.
Professor
Department of Science Education
University of Georgia
Athens, Georgia

Michael Padilla is a leader in middle school science education. He has served as an editor and elected officer for the National Science Teachers Association. He has been principal investigator of several National Science Foundation and Eisenhower grants and served as a writer of the National Science Education Standards.

As lead author of *Science Explorer,* Mike has inspired the team in developing a program that meets the needs of middle grades students, promotes science inquiry, and is aligned with the National Science Education Standards.

Ioannis Miaoulis, Ph.D.
Dean of Engineering
College of Engineering
Tufts University
Medford, Massachusetts

Martha Cyr, Ph.D.
Director, Engineering
    Educational Outreach
College of Engineering
Tufts University
Medford, Massachusetts

Science Explorer was created in collaboration with the College of Engineering at Tufts University. Tufts has an extensive engineering outreach program that uses engineering design and construction to excite and motivate students and teachers in science and technology education.

Faculty from Tufts University participated in the development of *Science Explorer* chapter projects, reviewed the student books for content accuracy, and helped coordinate field testing.

Book Authors

David V. Frank, Ph.D.
Head, Department of Physical Sciences
Ferris State University
Big Rapids, Michigan

John G. Little
Science Teacher
St. Mary's High School
Stockton, California

Steve Miller
Science Writer
State College, Pennsylvania

Contributing Writers

Thomas L. Messer
Science Teacher
Cape Cod Academy
Osterville, Massachusetts

Thomas R. Wellnitz
Science Teacher
The Paideia School
Atlanta, Georgia

Reading Consultant

Bonnie B. Armbruster, Ph.D.
Department of Curriculum
    and Instruction
University of Illinois
Champaign, Illinois

Interdisciplinary Consultant

Heidi Hayes Jacobs, Ed.D.
Teacher's College
Columbia University
New York, New York

Safety Consultants

W. H. Breazeale, Ph.D.
Department of Chemistry
College of Charleston
Charleston, South Carolina

Ruth Hathaway, Ph.D.
Hathaway Consulting
Cape Girardeau, Missouri

Teacher Reviewers

Stephanie Anderson
Sierra Vista Junior
    High School
Canyon Country, California

John W. Anson
Mesa Intermediate School
Palmdale, California

Pamela Arline
Lake Taylor Middle School
Norfolk, Virginia

Lynn Beason
College Station Jr. High School
College Station, Texas

Richard Bothmer
Hollis School District
Hollis, New Hampshire

Jeffrey C. Callister
Newburgh Free Academy
Newburgh, New York

Judy D'Albert
Harvard Day School
Corona Del Mar, California

Betty Scott Dean
Guilford County Schools
McLeansville, North Carolina

Sarah C. Duff
Baltimore City Public Schools
Baltimore, Maryland

Melody Law Ewey
Holmes Junior High School
Davis, California

Sherry L. Fisher
Lake Zurich Middle
    School North
Lake Zurich, Illinois

Melissa Gibbons
Fort Worth ISD
Fort Worth, Texas

Debra J. Goodding
Kraemer Middle School
Placentia, California

Jack Grande
Weber Middle School
Port Washington, New York

Steve Hills
Riverside Middle School
Grand Rapids, Michigan

Carol Ann Lionello
Kraemer Middle School
Placentia, California

Jaime A. Morales
Henry T. Gage Middle School
Huntington Park, California

Patsy Partin
Cameron Middle School
Nashville, Tennessee

Deedra H. Robinson
Newport News Public Schools
Newport News, Virginia

Bonnie Scott
Clack Middle School
Abilene, Texas

Charles M. Sears
Belzer Middle School
Indianapolis, Indiana

Barbara M. Strange
Ferndale Middle School
High Point, North Carolina

Jackie Louise Ulfig
Ford Middle School
Allen, Texas

Kathy Usina
Belzer Middle School
Indianapolis, Indiana

Heidi M. von Oetinger
L'Anse Creuse Public School
Harrison Township, Michigan

Pam Watson
Hill Country Middle School
Austin, Texas

Activity Field Testers

Nicki Bibbo
Russell Street School
Littleton, Massachusetts

Connie Boone
Fletcher Middle School
Jacksonville Beach, Florida

Rose-Marie Botting
Broward County
    School District
Fort Lauderdale, Florida

Colleen Campos
Laredo Middle School
Aurora, Colorado

Elizabeth Chait
W. L. Chenery Middle School
Belmont, Massachusetts

Holly Estes
Hale Middle School
Stow, Massachusetts

Laura Hapgood
Plymouth Community
    Intermediate School
Plymouth, Massachusetts

Sandra M. Harris
Winman Junior High School
Warwick, Rhode Island

Jason Ho
Walter Reed Middle School
Los Angeles, California

Joanne Jackson
Winman Junior High School
Warwick, Rhode Island

Mary F. Lavin
Plymouth Community
    Intermediate School
Plymouth, Massachusetts

James MacNeil, Ph.D.
Concord Public Schools
Concord, Massachusetts

Lauren Magruder
St. Michael's Country
    Day School
Newport, Rhode Island

Jeanne Maurand
Glen Urquhart School
Beverly Farms, Massachusetts

Warren Phillips
Plymouth Community
    Intermediate School
Plymouth, Massachusetts

Carol Pirtle
Hale Middle School
Stow, Massachusetts

Kathleen M. Poe
Kirby-Smith Middle School
Jacksonville, Florida

Cynthia B. Pope
Ruffner Middle School
Norfolk, Virginia

Anne Scammell
Geneva Middle School
Geneva, New York

Karen Riley Sievers
Callanan Middle School
Des Moines, Iowa

David M. Smith
Howard A. Eyer Middle School
Macungie, Pennsylvania

Derek Strohschneider
Plymouth Community
    Intermediate School
Plymouth, Massachusetts

Sallie Teames
Rosemont Middle School
Fort Worth, Texas

Gene Vitale
Parkland Middle School
McHenry, Illinois

Zenovia Young
Meyer Levin Junior
    High School (IS 285)
Brooklyn, New York

PRENTICE HALL
SCIENCE EXPLORER

Contents

Chemical Building Blocks

Activities

From Plants to CHEMICALS

Can you power a car with corn? Can you drink soda from a bottle made from plants? Can you use a farmer's corn crop to make chemicals strong enough to remove paint?

You can, thanks to scientists like Rathin Datta. Dr. Datta specializes in finding ways to get useful chemicals from plants. His discoveries will help make the environment cleaner for all of us.

Rathin is a chemical engineer at the Argonne National Laboratory in Illinois. For years, he has been finding ways to make useful products from substances found naturally in plants. He's helped find ways to turn corn into an automobile fuel called gasohol. He's researched plants that can be used to produce powerful medicines. He even worked on a way to use corn to make a stretchy fabric that athletes wear.

"I've always been interested in the plant and biological side of chemistry," says Rathin, who grew up in northern India. Even in grade school, he was interested in science. "That's because I've always been concerned about the effect of chemicals on the environment."

Rathin Datta was born in India, just north of Delhi. His interest in science was inspired in part by his father, who was a mathematician. Rathin came to the United States in 1970 to get a doctorate in chemical engineering at Princeton University. He works now at Argonne National Laboratory in Argonne, Illinois. In his free time, he enjoys tennis, hiking, and biking. He plays the sitar, an Indian lute, and has a special interest in opera.

Talking with Rathin Datta

Are Plant-Based Chemicals Safer?

Chemicals that come from crop plants are called *agrochemicals*, meaning "chemicals from agriculture," Rathin explains. Many agrochemicals are much less dangerous to the environment than chemicals made from petroleum. For one thing, although some agrochemicals can be poisonous to humans, most are not.

Because agrochemicals are made from plant materials, nature usually recycles them just as it recycles dead plants. Think of what happens to a tree after it falls to the ground. Tiny microbes work on its leaves and branches until the tree has rotted completely away. Much the same thing happens to products made from agrochemicals. A bag made from corn-based chemicals will break down and disappear after only a few weeks of being buried. In contrast, a plastic bag made from *petrochemicals*—chemicals made from petroleum—can survive hundreds of years.

Converting Carbohydrates

The starting ingredients in many agrochemicals are energy-rich substances called carbohydrates. Sugar and starch are carbohydrates. Rathin Datta converts, or changes, carbohydrates from corn into an agrochemical that can be used to make plastic. To do this, he needs help from tiny organisms—bacteria. First, he explains, he puts a special kind of bacteria in a big vat of ground-up corn. The bacteria convert the corn's carbohydrates into acids through a

Researchers Rathin Datta (right), Mike Henry (center), and Shih-Perng Tsai (left) developed the new, low-cost solvent. The dark substance is the fermented corn mixture. The clear substance that Rathin holds is the solvent.

natural process called fermentation. Rathin then uses the acids to make agrochemical plastic.

"The bacteria do all the work of converting the carbohydrates into useful molecules," says Rathin. "The hardest part for us comes afterward. The fermentation process produces a brew that contains a whole mix of materials. We have to find ways to separate out the one kind of material that we want to use from all the others."

This sign on a gasoline pump advertises gasohol.

Products That Can Be Made From Corn

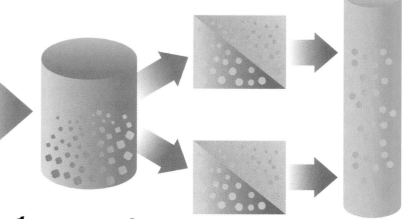

Corn Plant

Fermentation

Recovery and Purification

Making Paint Remover From Corn

Rathin Datta's most recent discovery is a good example of how agrochemicals can replace petrochemicals. He and his team have found a new way to use corn to make powerful solvents. Solvents are used to dissolve other substances.

"Solvents are found everywhere," says Rathin. "For example, factories use them in many processes to clean electronic parts or to remove ink from recycled newspapers. Households use them in grease-cleaning detergents and in paint removers."

Almost 4 million tons of solvents are used in the United States every year. Most are made from petrochemicals and can be very poisonous.

"Scientists have known for a long time that much safer solvents can be made from agrochemicals," says Rathin. "But the process has been too expensive. It doesn't do any good to make something that is environmentally sound if it costs too much for people to use," says Rathin. "Our challenge as chemical engineers

Spandex was used to make the blue tops these dancers are wearing.

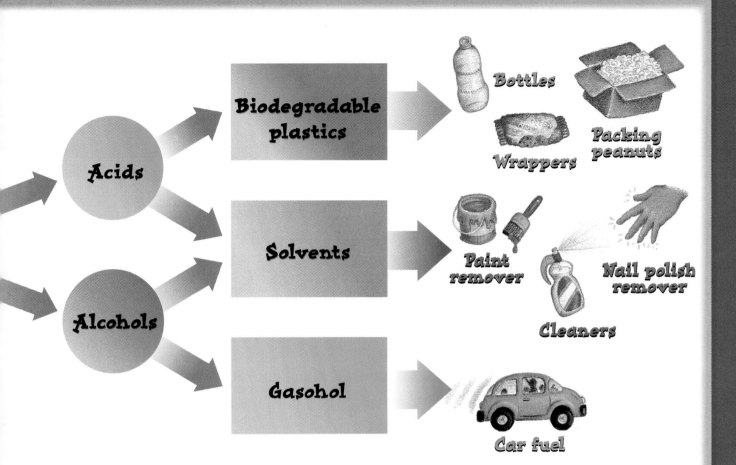

Acids

Alcohols

Biodegradable plastics

Bottles

Wrappers

Packing peanuts

Solvents

Paint remover

Nail polish remover

Cleaners

Gasohol

Car fuel

was to think about an old process in an entirely new way. We had to find a less expensive way to make these solvents."

Discovering a New Process

Rathin needed a new process to separate the solvents he wanted from a mixture. "I started working with a new kind of plastic that acts like a very fine filter. When we pass the fermented corn over this plastic, it captures the acids we want to keep and lets the other material pass through."

After two years of experimenting, Rathin perfected his process of making agrochemical solvents. His process works for less than half the cost of the old method. It also uses 90 percent less energy. Soon, most of the solvents used in the United States

could be this cleaner, safer kind made from corn. "It even makes a a great fingernail polish remover," says Datta.

"It's very satisfying to take a natural product like corn and use it to produce a chemical that will replace a less safe chemical," says Rathin. "It's rare to find a compound that can do everything that this corn solvent can do and still be nonpoisonous and easily break down in the environment."

In Your Journal

Rathin Datta and his team had discovered years ago how to make a solvent that was safer for the environment. But it was very expensive to make. Rathin could have stopped his research at that point. Instead, he chose to continue. What does this action tell you about how scientists like Datta meet challenges?

CHAPTER

1 An Introduction to Matter

Cooling lift

WHAT'S AHEAD

SECTION

1 Describing Matter

Discover **What Properties Help You Sort Matter?**
Sharpen Your Skills **Interpreting Data**
Try This **A Magnetic Personality**

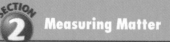

SECTION

2 Measuring Matter

Discover **Which Has More Mass?**
Try This **Bubble Time**
Skills Lab **Making Sense of Density**

SECTION

3 Particles of Matter

Discover **What's in the Box?**

Comparing Brand X

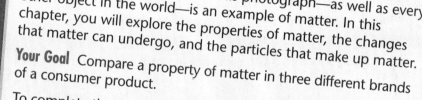

Antiques at a Virginia country store

Colored glass bottles, a wooden duck, a wicker chair, a doll and her dress, a metal pitcher and a watering can are for sale at a country store. These items and others in the photo provide just a glimpse of the huge variety of materials that make up our world. The scientific name for these materials is matter. Every object you see in this photograph—as well as every other object in the world—is an example of matter. In this chapter, you will explore the properties of matter, the changes that matter can undergo, and the particles that make up matter.

Your Goal Compare a property of matter in three different brands of a consumer product.

To complete the project you will
◆ design a comparison test on the products and collect data
◆ provide a procedure for your partner to follow
◆ conduct the comparison test designed by your partner
◆ compare the data you and your partner obtained
◆ follow the safety guidelines in Appendix A

Get Started As a class, brainstorm a list of different products to compare. For each product, write down several properties that could be compared. For example, paper towels may absorb different amounts of water or adhesive bandages may have different strengths. Review Designing an Experiment in the Skills Handbook.

Check Your Progress You'll be working on this project as you study this chapter. To keep your project on track, look for Check Your Progress boxes at the following points.
Section 1 Review, page 21: Design an experiment.
Section 3 Review, page 33: Perform the procedure.
Section 4 Review, page 38: Trade procedures with your partner.

Wrap Up At the end of the chapter (page 41), you and your partner will see if you can repeat each other's procedures.

SECTION 1 Describing Matter

DISCOVER •• ACTIVITY ••••

What Properties Help You Sort Matter?

1. Carefully examine the ten objects that your teacher provides. Write a brief description of each object. What properties are unique to each object? What properties do some objects have in common?

2. Which objects appear to be made of a single substance? Which objects appear to be mixtures of different substances?

3. Divide the objects into small groups so that the objects in each group share one of the properties you identified.

Think It Over

Classifying Share your observations and grouping with your classmates. How do the ways your classmates grouped the objects compare with the way you grouped the objects? Think of at least one other way to group the objects.

GUIDE FOR READING

◆ **What are the three states of matter?**

◆ **Why are characteristic properties useful?**

◆ **How can matter be classified?**

Reading Tip As you read, make a list of properties of matter.

You probably have heard the word *matter* used in lots of ways. "It doesn't matter!" "As a matter of fact, . . ." "Hey, what's the matter?"

In science, however, the word *matter* has a specific meaning. Matter is the "stuff" that makes up everything in the universe. Fruit, baseballs, statues, milk, books, flowers: These objects and countless others are examples of matter. Even air is matter. Air may be invisible, but you know it is there when you feel a cool breeze or watch trees bend in the wind.

What exactly is matter? This question is not so easy to answer! You can begin by looking at some of its properties.

Properties of Matter

Matter might be hard or soft, rough or smooth, round or square, hot or cold. Some matter may catch fire easily, while other matter does not. It may fit inside a shoebox or be as big as the entire Earth!

Figure 1 A geyser gives off hot water and steam—small droplets of hot liquid water in air. A geyser also gives off water vapor. In cold air, the invisible water vapor quickly turns to more droplets of steam, adding to the drama of the scene.

Matter may be any color of the rainbow—or no color at all. Hardness, texture, shape, temperature, flammability, size, and color are all examples of properties of matter.

Can matter change properties? The answer is yes. Water, for example, is a clear liquid at room temperature. At cold temperatures, however, water is in its solid form—ice—which is hard and frosty. And at high temperatures, water exists in the form of water vapor, which is an invisible gas. In Figure 1 you can see evidence of water in its solid and liquid forms.

Liquid water, ice, and water vapor are all made of exactly the same substance, but in different states. **Solids, liquids, and gases are the three principal states of matter.** You will learn much more about these three states of matter in Chapter 2.

Characteristic Properties

Some properties of matter, such as size or amount, are true only for a given sample of matter. For example, a piece of ice can be as small as an ice cube or as big as a glacier. In both cases, the substance is still ice. However, some properties hold true for a particular kind of substance no matter what the sample. These properties are called **characteristic properties.** For example, all diamonds have the same hardness. (In fact, they are the hardest of all known substances.) **Since characteristic properties for a given substance never change, they can be used to identify unknown matter.**

ACTIVITY

Look at the melting points and boiling points of the five substances listed in the table. Identify each substance's physical state at room temperature (approximately 20°C). Is it a gas, a liquid, or a solid? Explain how you arrived at your conclusions.

Substance	Melting Point (°C)	Boiling Point (°C)
Water	0	100
Chloroform	−64	61
Ethanol	−117	79
Propane	−190	−42
Table salt	801	1,465

Figure 2 All pure substances, including frozen water, melt at a characteristic temperature.

Boiling Point If you put a pan of water on a stove and turn on the burner, the water soon begins to boil. Can you predict the temperature at which the water boils? Typically, the answer is 100°C (100 degrees Celsius). You can repeat this activity as many times as you like, and each time the water will boil at almost exactly the same temperature. However, if you try boiling other liquids, such as vegetable oil or melted margarine, you will find that they boil at very different temperatures from water.

The temperature at which a liquid boils is called its **boiling point.** Boiling point is an example of a characteristic property of a substance. For this reason, comparing boiling points can be an excellent way to tell one liquid from another. For example, consider three different liquids: water, chloroform, and ethanol. Chloroform once was used to put people to sleep in operating rooms, and ethanol is one of a group of substances called alcohols. All three liquids are clear and colorless—you would not be able to tell them apart from their looks alone. But look at the table shown to the left, and you will see that each liquid boils at a different temperature.

Melting Point Another characteristic property can help you identify solids. Suppose you removed a tray of ice cubes from a freezer whose temperature is about −10°C and placed it in a warm kitchen whose temperature is about 25°C. The ice cubes would gradually warm. When their temperature reached 0°C, they would begin to melt. The temperature at which a solid melts is called its **melting point.** Because a solid substance melts at one temperature only, melting point is another characteristic property.

Not all solids melt as readily as ice. If you heated a sample of table salt, it wouldn't melt until the temperature was more than 800°C. That's hotter than the highest setting on most ovens!

If you have a solid that melts at 0°C, can you be sure that it's water? Not necessarily! Other solids melt at 0°C, also. In fact, many substances share melting points, boiling points, or other characteristic properties. For this reason, you sometimes need to study at least two or three characteristic properties before you can accurately identify a substance.

☑ *Checkpoint* *What are two examples of characteristic properties?*

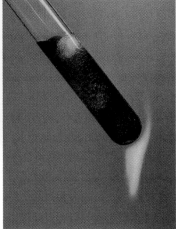

Figure 3 Unlike a physical change, a chemical change alters the identity of a substance. In a forest fire, wood is changed into gases and other substances. In a test tube, caramel can be produced by heating sugar. *Observing How can you tell that new substances were formed in both photos?*

Changes in Matter

Changes in the state of matter, such as boiling or melting, are examples of physical changes. **Physical changes** alter the form of a substance, but not its identity. Even when you boil away a pan of water, the water is still present as water vapor. Other examples of physical changes include crushing a soda can, tearing a piece of paper, and mixing sugar into iced tea or breakfast cereal. Separating the parts of a substance, such as filtering orange juice to remove the pulp, is also a physical change. In each of these examples, the form or appearance of the substances changed, but the substances themselves remained.

In **chemical changes,** however, one or more substances combine or break apart to form new substances. Heating table sugar and changing it into caramel is one example of a chemical change. When this process is complete, the original sugar particles no longer exist. Burning wood is another example of a chemical change. When wood burns, it combines with oxygen in the air to produce the glowing gases that you recognize as fire. This process changes the wood into ash and gases that are no longer wood.

The ability of a substance to undergo a specific chemical change is another example of a characteristic property. This property is called the **chemical activity** of the substance.

Figure 4 These two students are conducting a taste test to try to identify different drinks. *Predicting* Explain why you think they will or will not be able to do so.

A Magnetic Personality

How can you separate the substances in a mixture?

ACTIVITY

1. Obtain a mixture of sand and iron filings. Place the mixture in the center of a piece of paper.

2. Examine the mixture carefully. Predict the effect a magnet would have on it.

3. Hold a magnet below the paper under the mixture. Move the magnet toward the edge of the paper.

4. Use the magnet to separate as much of the mixture as you can.

Inferring Was your prediction in Step 2 correct? How do the two parts of the mixture differ? What characteristic property allowed you to separate parts of the mixture?

Types of Matter

Why do fruit juices taste different? The answer is that they contain different ingredients. Put another way, the matter in each juice is different. Scientists sometimes find it useful to describe matter in terms of its composition. **Matter can be classified into two general categories: mixtures and pure substances. The pure substances include elements and compounds.**

Mixtures

What exactly is in the drinks shown in Figure 4? Each of them contains many ingredients, including water, sugar, flavorings, and maybe bits of pulp from fruit. These drinks are examples of mixtures. A **mixture** consists of two or more substances that are mixed together but not chemically combined.

In a mixture the individual substances keep their separate properties. It may not be easy to see the sugar in orange or grape juice, but you certainly can taste it! Sometimes, you can easily separate the substances that make up a mixture. If you boil sea water, for example, you can separate the salt and water that compose it.

Scientists often classify mixtures by how "well-mixed" they are. In mixtures like sea water, the parts have blended so well together that they appear to be a single substance. Sea water is a mixture of water, salt, and other substances. This type of mixture is called a solution. You can think of a **solution** as the "best-mixed" of all possible mixtures. Sugar water is another example of a solution.

☑ *Checkpoint* How are solutions related to mixtures?

Pure Substances

Not every substance is a mixture. If you could look closely enough at sugar, for example—down to the level of the tiny particles that it is made of—you would see that sugar is a pure substance, with no other substances mixed in. A **pure substance** is made of only one kind of matter and has definite properties. Examples of pure substances include sugar, salt, iron, aluminum, and copper.

Every sample of a pure substance is always the same, no matter what the form. For example, if you separated all the ingredients from different kinds of fruit juices, the water from each juice would be exactly the same. So would the water from tap water, sea water, and blood. Water can be mixed with all sorts of other substances, but water itself is always the same substance.

Elements Some pure substances, called **elements,** cannot be broken down into other substances by any chemical means. Individually or in combination, the elements form every object in the world around you! You might be surprised to learn that there are only a little more than 100 different elements. And of these, you probably use only 30 or 40 in your daily life.

Take a look at the list of the chemical elements shown in Appendix C. Notice that most elements are represented by a one-letter or two-letter symbol—for example, C for carbon and Cl for chlorine. How many of the elements do you recognize? Many of the familiar elements are metals, such as iron (the main ingredient in steel), and copper (used in electrical wiring). Nitrogen and oxygen are two elements that are part of the air you breathe.

Figure 5 The element silver (above) sometimes is found as pure metal having a wiry, treelike form. You can see compounds and mixtures anywhere you look. The trees, other plants, and pond water in a quiet garden (left) are made of mixtures of compounds containing carbon, hydrogen, oxygen, and a few other elements.

EXPLORING *Matter at the Beach*

You can find all sorts of matter at an ocean beach, including sand, sea shells, grasses and other plants, and sea water. Many types of beach sand are made up of small rocks and other particles that are washed ashore by the ocean's waves.

Mixture
Some beach sand is a mixture of a substance called quartz and tiny fragments of sea shells. The color of the beach sand varies with its shell content.

Compounds
Sea shells contain different calcium compounds, including calcium carbonate. Quartz is formed from a compound called silicon dioxide.

Calcium carbonate

Silicon dioxide

Elements
The compounds in beach sand are made mostly of four elements: silicon, oxygen, calcium, and carbon. Like most substances, beach sand shares few properties with the elements that compose it!

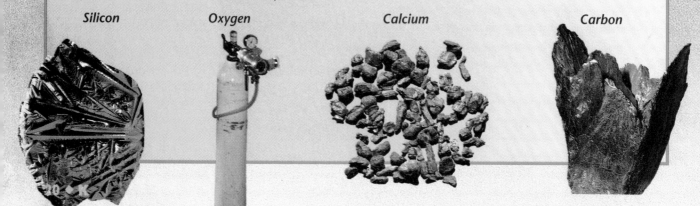

Silicon   *Oxygen*   *Calcium*   *Carbon*

Compounds How can just a little more than 100 elements make up all the matter in the universe? The answer is that the elements combine in different ways to form a huge variety of compounds. A **compound** is a pure substance formed from chemical combinations of two or more different elements. Water and carbon dioxide are examples of compounds. Just as symbols are used to represent elements, formulas are used to represent compounds. Water's formula is H_2O and carbon dioxide's formula is CO_2.

The properties of compounds are always different from the properties of the elements that formed them. For example, the element carbon (C) typically exists as a powdery, black solid. The elements hydrogen (H) and oxygen (O) exist as invisible gases. When these elements combine to form compounds, however, the result is a different substance. One compound of carbon, hydrogen, and oxygen is ordinary table sugar, a granular, white solid. Its formula is $C_{12}H_{22}O_{11}$. The properties of table sugar are very different from those of the elements that formed it.

Matter Is All Around You

Now that you've read this section, choose some familiar objects and ask yourself some questions about them. Are the objects solids, liquids, or gases? Which are mixtures and which are pure substances? Can you identify any of the elements you read about, such as oxygen, iron, copper, or aluminum? By asking questions and paying attention to the answers, you are taking the first steps in the study of matter—the "stuff" that makes up everything in the universe.

Figure 6 You interact with matter all the time, whether you are riding a bike, eating a sandwich, or making a giant soap bubble!

Section 1 Review

1. List the three principal states of matter. Give two examples of each.
2. What is meant by a characteristic property of a substance?
3. Compare physical changes and chemical changes. Use examples in your answer.
4. Describe how matter is classified into mixtures, pure substances, elements, and compounds.
5. **Thinking Critically Applying Concepts** Liquid A and Liquid B both boil at 100°C. Using what you know about characteristic properties, explain why the liquids may not be the same.

Check Your Progress
CHAPTER PROJECT 1

Choose which product and property you will test. Design a procedure to test your chosen property of a product. Decide which variables you will keep constant. Describe how you will measure and organize the data you will collect. Work with a partner to discuss ideas for your procedure. Answer your partner's questions about the procedure, listen to any comments offered, and incorporate appropriate comments into your plan.

SECTION 2 Measuring Matter

DISCOVER ······························· ACTIVITY

Which Has More Mass?

1. Your teacher will provide you with some small objects, such as a rock, a plastic drinking cup, an aluminum can, and a pencil. Look at the objects, but do not touch them.

2. Predict which object is lightest, which is second lightest, and so on. Record your predictions.

3. Use a triple-beam balance to find the mass of each object.

4. Based on your results, list the objects from lightest to heaviest.

Think It Over

Drawing Conclusions How did your predictions compare to your results? Are bigger objects always heavier than smaller objects? Why or why not?

GUIDE FOR READING

◆ What is the difference between weight and mass?

◆ How is density calculated?

Reading Tip Before you read, define mass, volume, and density in your own words. Then revise your definitions as you read.

Figure 7 If a dog won't stand on the scale by itself, you can step on the scale with it.

Here's a riddle for you: Which weighs more, a pound of feathers or a pound of bricks? If you answered "the pound of bricks," think again. Both weigh exactly the same—one pound!

There are all sorts of ways of measuring matter, and you use these measurements every day. Scientists rely on measurements as well. In fact, scientists work hard to make sure that their measurements are as accurate as possible.

Mass

A veterinarian wants an updated weight for a dog at its annual check-up. To find the weight, the owner steps on the scale in the vet's office, holding the dog. Their combined body weight presses down on springs inside the scale. The more the girl or her dog weighs, the more the springs compress and the higher the reading. Subtract the owner's weight from the total, and the vet has his answer.

However, a scale would not indicate the same weight if you were on the moon. Step on a scale on the moon, and the springs inside it wouldn't compress as much as they did on Earth. You would weigh less on the moon.

22 ◆ K

Weight or Mass? Why does your weight change when you travel away from Earth? The reason is that your **weight** is a measure of the force of gravity on you. On Earth, all objects are attracted downward by Earth's gravity. On other planets, the force of gravity may be more or less. On the moon, the force of gravity is much weaker than on Earth. You weigh less.

In everyday life, weight is a useful measurement of how much matter an object contains. But scientists rely on a property that is constant wherever the object may be. This property is called mass. The **mass** of an object is the measurement of how much matter it contains. **An object's weight will change if you move it from Earth to the moon or to other planets, but its mass will stay the same.**

Units of Mass To measure the properties of matter, scientists use a system of units called the **International System of Units.** The system is abbreviated "SI," after its French name, Système International. For mass, the SI unit is the kilogram (kg). If you weigh 90 pounds on Earth, then your mass is approximately 40 kilograms.

Although you sometimes will see kilograms used in this textbook, usually you will see a smaller unit—the gram (g). There are exactly 1,000 grams in a kilogram. A nickel has a mass of about 5 grams, the mass of a baseball is about 150 grams, and the water in a medium-sized glass has a mass of about 200 grams.

☑ *Checkpoint* *What is the SI unit for mass?*

Volume

The amount of space that matter occupies is called its **volume.** It's easy to see the volume that solid and liquid objects take up. But gases have volume, too. Watch a balloon as you blow into it. You're actually increasing its volume with your breath.

Bubble Time

Do gases have volume?

1. Fill a large container with water. Completely submerge a clear plastic cup, right side up, in the container.
2. Mark the water level with a piece of tape on the outside of the container.
3. Turn the cup upside down underwater, without letting any air bubbles enter the cup.
4. Insert the short end of the straw into the water and up into the cup. Then blow into the straw.

Inferring Did blowing air into the cup change the water level in the container? Explain your observations.

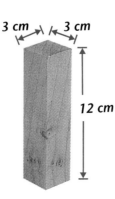

Figure 8 Volume is measured in several units. Usually, liquids are measured in liters (L) or milliliters (mL), and solids are measured in cubic centimeters (cm^3).

> **INTEGRATING MATHEMATICS**

For rectangular objects such as a block of wood, the volume is found by multiplying the measurements of length, width, and height.

$$Volume = Length \times Width \times Height$$

When you multiply the three measurements, you must multiply the units as well as the numbers. So, just as $2 \times 2 \times 2 = 2^3$, $cm \times cm \times cm = cm^3$. If a block of wood has a length of 3 centimeters, a width of 3 centimeters, and a height of 12 centimeters, then the volume would equal the product of those values.

$$Volume = 3\,cm \times 3\,cm \times 12\,cm = 108\,cm^3$$

Measurement Systems

Like so much else in science, systems of measurement developed gradually over time in different parts of the world.

1400 B.C.

Egypt

The ancient Egyptians developed the first known weighing instrument, a simple balance with a pointer. Earlier, they had been the first to standardize a measure of length. The length, called a cubit, was originally defined as the distance between the elbow and the tip of the middle finger.

| 1500 B.C. | 1000 B.C. | 500 B.C. | A.D. 1 |

640 B.C

Lydia

Merchants in the Middle East and Mediterranean used units of weight to be sure that they received the correct amount of gold and silver and to check the purity of the metal. A *talent* was about 25 kilograms and a *mina* about 500 grams. The Lydians minted the first true coins to have standard weight and value.

200 B.C

China

Shih Huang Ti, the first emperor of China, set standards for weight, length, and volume. Even earlier, the Chinese were the first to use decimal notation, the number system based on 10 digits. This is the system most people use today.

The name for cm³ is the cubic centimeter, and it is a common unit of volume. Other units of volume include the liter (L) and the milliliter (mL), both of which are often used to measure liquids. A milliliter is exactly 1 cubic centimeter. There are 1,000 milliliters in one liter.

How can you measure the volume of an object with an irregular shape, such as a piece of fruit or a rock? One way is to put the object in a graduated cylinder containing water and measure the change in the volume of the water.

☑ *Checkpoint* *How can you calculate the volume of a rectangular object like a shoebox?*

In Your Journal

Although scientists rely on SI units, people use other measurement units for many different purposes. Research the units used in diamond cutting, horse breeding, sailing, or other activities that interest you. Write a brief essay to present your findings.

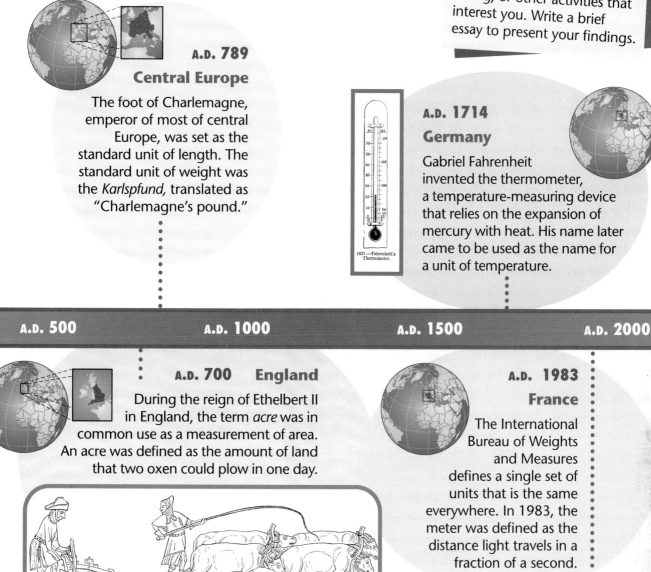

A.D. 789
Central Europe

The foot of Charlemagne, emperor of most of central Europe, was set as the standard unit of length. The standard unit of weight was the *Karlspfund,* translated as "Charlemagne's pound."

A.D. 1714
Germany

Gabriel Fahrenheit invented the thermometer, a temperature-measuring device that relies on the expansion of mercury with heat. His name later came to be used as the name for a unit of temperature.

1531.—Fahrenheit's Thermometer.

A.D. 500   **A.D. 1000**   **A.D. 1500**   **A.D. 2000**

A.D. 700   **England**

During the reign of Ethelbert II in England, the term *acre* was in common use as a measurement of area. An acre was defined as the amount of land that two oxen could plow in one day.

A.D. 1983
France

The International Bureau of Weights and Measures defines a single set of units that is the same everywhere. In 1983, the meter was defined as the distance light travels in a fraction of a second.

Figure 9 This table lists commonly-used units of mass, volume, and distance. *Making Generalizations Which units measure the amount of space an object occupies? Which units measure the amount of matter in an object?*

Common Units and Conversions			
Quantity	SI/Metric Units	Other Units	Conversions
Mass	Kilogram (kg) Gram (g)		1 kilogram = 1,000 grams
Volume	Cubic meter (m³) Liter (L) Milliliter (mL) Cubic centimeter (cm³)	Quart Gallon	1 milliliter = 1 cm³
Distance	Meter (m) Kilometer (km) Centimeter (cm)	Foot Mile Inch	1 kilometer = 1,000 meters 1 centimeter = 0.01 meter

Density

Different substances may have the same mass, but they don't necessarily fill the same volume. Remember the riddle about the bricks and the feathers? A kilogram of bricks takes up a much smaller volume than the same mass of feathers. This is because bricks and feathers have different densities—a very important characteristic property of matter. **Density** is the measurement of how much mass is contained in a given volume. **To calculate the density of an object, divide its mass by its volume.**

$$Density = \frac{Mass}{Volume}$$

Figure 10 An object sinks or floats depending, in part, on its density. These ducks are made of many different substances, but overall, a duck's body has a density less than that of water.

A unit of density is always a unit of mass, such as grams, divided by a unit of volume, such as cubic centimeters. One typical unit of density is written as "g/cm³," which is read as "grams per cubic centimeter." The word *per* means "for each," which in mathematics is the same as "divided by." For liquids, density is often stated in grams per milliliter, or g/mL. The density of water is 1.0 g/mL, which is the same as 1.0 g/cm³.

Sometimes you can compare the densities of substances just by observing them. For example, suppose you have a solid block of wood and a solid block of gold. When you drop each block into a tub of water, the wood floats and the gold sinks. You know the density of water is 1.0 g/cm³. You can conclude that the wood has a density lower than 1.0 g/cm³. In contrast, the density of the gold is greater than 1.0 g/cm³.

Sample Problem

A small block of wood floats on water. It has a volume of 25 cubic centimeters and a mass of 20 grams. What is the density of the wood?

Analyze. You know the mass and the volume. You want to find the density.

Write the formula.
$$\text{Density} = \frac{\text{Mass}}{\text{Volume}}$$

Substitute and solve.
$$\text{Density} = \frac{20\ g}{25\ cm^3}$$
$$\text{Density} = 0.8\ g/cm^3$$

Think about it. The answer shows mass per unit volume. The correct unit is g/cm^3.

Practice Problems

1. A sample of liquid has a mass of 24 grams and a volume of 16 milliliters. What is the density of the liquid?
2. A metal sample has a mass of 43.5 grams and a volume of 15 cubic centimeters. What is its density?

Watch a bottle of oil-and-vinegar salad dressing after it's been shaken. You will see oil droplets rise toward the top of the bottle. Eventually, the oil forms a separate layer above the other ingredients. What can you conclude? You're right if you said the oil is less dense than the rest of the liquid dressing.

The density of a substance is the same for all samples of that substance. For example, all samples of pure gold have a density of 19.3 g/cm^3. Therefore, density is another example of a characteristic property.

Section 2 Review

1. Why are mass and weight different measurements?
2. What two quantities do you need to know in order to calculate density?
3. Describe how you could measure the volume of an object with an irregular shape.
4. **Thinking Critically Problem Solving** The density of aluminum is 2.7 g/cm^3. A metal sample has a mass of 52.0 grams and a volume of 17.1 cubic centimeters. Could the sample be aluminum? Explain your answer.

Science at Home

You can demonstrate differences in density to your family. Label two cups A and B and place a cup of water in each. Stir 3 teaspoons of salt and several drops of food coloring into Cup B. Dip a clear straw into Cup A to a depth of about 2 cm. Place your finger on the end of the straw and dip it into Cup B to a depth of about 4 cm. Remove your finger from the straw and then replace it. Remove the straw from the cup. Explain to your family what densities have to do with the results.

Skills Lab

MAKING SENSE OF DENSITY

If you break an object in half, does its density change? In this lab, you will compare the densities of objects of different sizes.

Problem

Is density a characteristic property of a substance?

Materials

balance   water   paper towels
wooden stick, approximately 6 cm long
ball of modeling clay, approximately 5 cm wide
crayon with paper covering removed
graduated cylinder, 100 mL

Procedure

1. Use a balance to find the mass of the wooden stick. Record the mass in a data table like the one at the right.
2. Add enough water to a graduated cylinder that the stick can be completely submerged. Measure the initial volume of the water.
3. Place the stick in the graduated cylinder. Measure the new volume of the water.
4. The volume of the stick is the difference between the water levels in Steps 2 and 3. Calculate this volume and record it.
5. The density of the stick equals its mass divided by its volume. Calculate and record the density.
6. Thoroughly dry the stick with a paper towel. Then carefully break the stick into two pieces. Repeat Steps 1 through 5 to calculate the density of each of the two pieces.
7. Repeat Steps 1 through 6 using the clay rolled into a rope.
8. Repeat again using the crayon.

Analyze and Conclude

1. For each of the three objects you tested, compare the density of the whole object with the densities of the pieces of the object.
2. Use your results to explain how density can be used to identify a substance.
3. Why did you dry the objects in Step 6?
4. **Think About It** Predict the results of this experiment if you had used a pencil that had an eraser on one end instead of a wooden stick. Explain your prediction.

More to Explore

Wrap the modeling clay around the wooden stick and predict the density of the object you created. Then measure mass and volume and calculate the density to see if your prediction was correct.

DATA TABLE

Object	Mass (g)	Volume Change (cm^3)	Density (g/cm^3)
Wooden Stick			
Whole			
Piece 1			
Piece 2			
Modeling Clay			
Whole			
Piece 1			
Piece 2			
Crayon			
Whole			
Piece 1			
Piece 2			

SECTION 3 Particles of Matter

DISCOVER ·············· ACTIVITY

What's in the Box?

1. Your teacher will give you a sealed box that contains one or more objects. Without opening the box, try to find out as much as you can about its contents. Try tilting, turning, shaking, or tapping the box.

2. Ask yourself questions such as these: Are the objects inside round or flat? Do they slide or roll? How many objects are there?

3. Make a list of your observations about the objects in the box.

4. Trade boxes with another group of students and repeat the activity.

Think It Over

Inferring Try to imagine what familiar objects would fit your observations. Make a sketch showing what you think the contents look like. How is it possible to make an inference from indirect evidence?

Glance at the painting below and you see people enjoying an afternoon in the park. Look again and you will notice that some of the people are in the sunlight and others are in the shade. How did the artist make your eyes see bright light, dark shadows, and shades between? The answer comes from a close look at a detail of the painting. The artist used many small spots of color to make his painting.

Are you surprised that small spots of color combine to make you see the people in the park on a sunny day? Believe it or not, all the matter in the universe is formed in a way that's not much different.

GUIDE FOR READING

◆ What are the smallest particles of an element?

◆ What did Dalton conclude about atoms?

Reading Tip As you read, outline the main points under each heading of the section.

◀ "Sunday Afternoon on the Island of La Grand Jatte," by Georges Seurat, at the Art Institute of Chicago

Chapter 1 **K ◆ 29**

Figure 11 A drop of spilled mercury breaks into droplets. (But don't try this at home. Mercury is poisonous and can cause brain damage.) Although these mercury droplets are small, they are not the smallest particles of mercury possible. *Applying Concepts What is the smallest particle of an element?*

Atoms

Is there a smallest possible piece of matter? To find out, you might tear a sheet of aluminum foil in half, and then tear the halves into quarters and tear the quarters into eighths.

Do you think you could tear the aluminum foil forever, always producing smaller and smaller pieces? Or do you think that you eventually would have the smallest possible piece?

If you have ever wondered about questions like these, you are not alone. Philosophers and scientists have asked questions like these for more than 2,000 years. Today, however, scientists state with certainty that aluminum is composed of extremely small particles called **atoms,** as are all other elements. **Atoms are the smallest particles of an element.**

Democritus

Figure 12 This statue of Democritus was made in ancient Rome many years after Democritus lived.

One of the first people known to have developed the idea of atoms did so quite a long time ago . . . about 440 B.C.! Democritus, a Greek philosopher, suggested that there were smallest possible "pieces" of everything, and that these pieces couldn't be divided any further. He thought that you could chop matter into ever smaller pieces until you got to its smallest piece. Democritus called this smallest piece *atomos,* which is Greek for "uncuttable." Does that word look familiar? Of course! It is the origin of the English word "atom."

Few other ancient Greek philosophers accepted the idea of atoms. And Democritus' idea that sweet objects have smooth atoms while sour-tasting objects have sharp atoms has no scientific basis. But over 2,000 years later, the ancient name is used for atoms today.

Dalton's Ideas

In 1802, an atomic theory was proposed by a British school teacher, John Dalton. No one knows how much Dalton was influenced by the ideas of Democritus. Unlike the ancient Greeks, Dalton carried out experiments in a laboratory.

Based on the evidence he had, Dalton inferred that atoms had to have certain characteristics. Here are the main ones.

♦ *Atoms can't be broken into smaller pieces.* **Dalton imagined atoms to be like tiny marbles, or rigid spheres that are impossible to break.**

♦ *In any element, all the atoms are exactly alike.* This idea explains why an element always has the same properties.

♦ *Atoms of two or more elements can combine to form compounds.* Because compounds could be broken down into elements, Dalton concluded that compounds are made of atoms as well.

♦ *Atoms of each element have a unique mass.* However, Dalton and other scientists of his day were not actually able to measure the mass of individual atoms.

♦ *The masses of the elements in a compound are always in a constant ratio.* Water, for example, is a compound composed of hydrogen atoms and oxygen atoms. If you compare any sample of pure water to any other sample of pure water, the ratio of the mass of hydrogen to the mass of oxygen is always the same.

Today, scientists have identified some important exceptions to Dalton's statements. Even so, Dalton's ideas form the basis of our understanding of atoms.

☑ *Checkpoint* *What were two of Dalton's ideas about atoms?*

Math TOOLBOX

Constant Ratios

A ratio is two quantities represented as a fraction. If two pairs of numbers produce the same ratio, the ratio is constant. Suppose you want to compare the ratio of 16 to 2 with the ratio of 24 to 3.

1. Write the first fraction, then reduce it to smallest whole-number values.

$$\frac{16}{2} = \frac{8}{1}$$

2. Now do the same with the other pair of numbers.

$$\frac{24}{3} = \frac{8}{1}$$

3. Both fractions produce the same ratio, so the ratio is constant.

In any sample of a compound, the ratio of the masses of two elements in the compound is always constant.

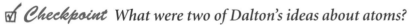

Figure 13 Calcium oxide, also called lime, is an ingredient in mortar—the "glue" that holds bricks together. In any amount of calcium oxide, the ratio of the mass of calcium to the mass of oxygen is always 5 to 2.

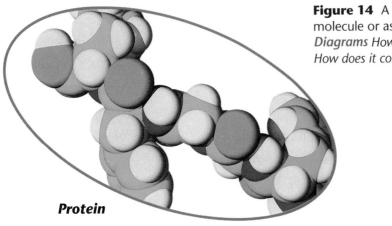

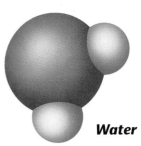

Figure 14 A molecule can be as complex as a protein molecule or as simple as a water molecule. *Interpreting Diagrams How many atoms are in the water molecule? How does it compare to the protein molecule?*

Protein

Water

Atoms and Molecules Today

Just as spots of color can be combined and arranged to form different pictures, so can atoms combine and arrange to form different compounds. In many cases, the basic particle of a compound is called a molecule. A **molecule** is a group of atoms that are joined together and act as a single unit. The force that holds two atoms together is called a **chemical bond.** Most atoms readily form chemical bonds with one or more other atoms.

Molecules can contain as many as a billion atoms or as few as two atoms. One of the simplest molecules is the water molecule (H_2O), shown in Figure 14. If you could look closely enough at a single drop of water, you would discover that it contains a huge number of water molecules. If you looked even closer, you would find that all the water molecules are the same, consisting of two hydrogen atoms and one oxygen atom.

How Small Is Small? Just how small are atoms? The best way to answer that question is to compare atoms to everyday objects. Here are some examples:

A sheet of paper is about 10,000 atoms thick.

There are 2,000,000,000,000,000,000,000 (that's 2,000 billion billion) atoms of oxygen in one drop of water—and twice as many atoms of hydrogen!

Newspaper pictures are made from tiny dots of ink. Each dot contains about a billion billion atoms! (That's a 1 followed by 18 zeros!)

Atoms are so small that for many years no one expected to see them. But now there is a tool that provides a glimpse of what atoms look like. The tool is called a scanning tunneling microscope. It can magnify things so much that it can actually capture images of atoms. Figure 15 shows an example of what the scanning tunneling microscope can reveal.

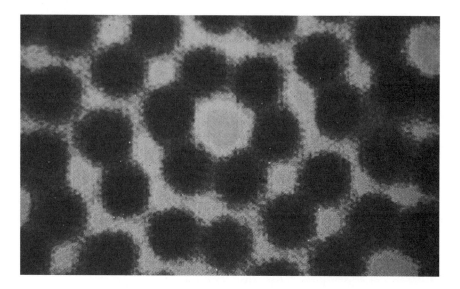

Figure 15 A scanning tunneling microscope produced this image of silicon atoms.

Using Models When you think about matter in terms of atoms and molecules, you are using a model known as the particle model of matter. A model is a mental picture of how things actually work.

The particle model is useful because it explains many facts about the world around you. In fact, scientists can explain all sorts of properties of the elements from studying the atoms that compose them. And they can explain the properties of compounds by studying the molecules that compose them.

Section 3 Review

1. What would you get if you could break an element into its smallest particles?

2. What did Dalton visualize atoms to be like?

3. An ice cube consists of molecules of water (H_2O). Could you continue, forever, to break an ice cube into smaller and smaller pieces of ice? Explain your answer.

4. **Thinking Critically Applying Concepts** The ancient Greek philosopher Aristotle argued against Democritus' ideas about atoms. "If matter is composed of indivisible particles," he asked, "then what holds these particles together?" Can you suggest an answer to Aristotle's question?

5. **Thinking Critically Calculating** A sample of a compound contains 64 grams of copper and 16 grams of oxygen. What is the ratio of the mass of copper to the mass of oxygen? If another sample of the compound has 40 grams of copper, how much oxygen is there in the second sample?

CHAPTER PROJECT 1

Check Your Progress

Have your teacher approve your procedure for testing your product. Then obtain the materials you need and perform the test. If you alter the procedure, change the instructions to reflect your alterations. (*Hint:* A good experimental procedure should be reliable. Test more than one sample of the same product to see if your results can be repeated.)

SECTION 4 Elements From Earth

How Can You Separate Bolts From Sand?

1. Mix dry sand with a few small metal bolts. Place the mixture in a tray or pie pan.

2. Think of a way to separate the sand and the bolts. You may not use a magnet, but may use water, a bowl, paper towels, and other supplies available in your classroom.

3. With your teacher's permission, try your procedure.

Think It Over

Designing an Experiment What properties of matter did you use to separate the sand and the bolts? How successful was your procedure?

GUIDE FOR READING

◆ What property of gold allows it to be panned?

◆ What property is used to extract copper or iron from their ores?

Reading Tip As you read, list the ways that people separate pure elements from the forms in which they are found in nature.

G old! In 1848, several gold nuggets were found in the American River in northern California near a mill owned by John Sutter. Thousands of people rushed to the California hills with pans, pickaxes, and shovels, hoping to find this precious metal. They searched the riverbanks and stream beds for more nuggets and even for flakes of gold. Some were lucky and got rich, but many returned home empty-handed. Perhaps the most disappointed of all were the people who found pyrite, a compound made of the elements iron and sulfur that looks like gold. Another name for pyrite is "fool's gold."

A gold miner pans for gold in Northern California. ▶

Gold and Density

Miners during the California gold rush took advantage of a characteristic property of the metal. As mentioned in Section 2, gold's density is 19.3 g/cm^3. This is much denser than the sand and dirt with which the gold is mixed. And the density of the look-alike pyrite is only 5.0 g/cm^3. **The high density of gold can be used to separate it from any surrounding material.**

Figure 16 Gold nuggets contain only the pure element gold.

Miners used the technique of panning to separate the gold from the sand and dirt with which the gold was mixed. They put a mixture of gold dust and sand and dirt into a shallow pan and covered it with water. When the water was swirled around the pan and then slowly poured out, the water tended to carry the less dense sand and dirt with it. The more dense gold sank and was left behind. This process was repeated until only pure gold dust remained in the bottom of the pan.

Today, gold mining is done on a much larger scale using big machines called dredges. However, the basic principle of separating gold by density is the same. The dredge scrapes up large amounts of sand and dirt, washes it with water, and separates the gold in a way similar to panning.

✓ *Checkpoint* *Why is the density of gold a characteristic property?*

Copper and Electrolysis

Gold nuggets and gold dust are almost pure gold. Other useful metals usually do not exist in nature as pure elements. Copper, for example, most often exists as a compound. Copper compounds are found in nature in certain rocks. A rock that contains a metal or other economically useful material is called an **ore.**

You cannot separate copper from its ore by breaking the ore into smaller pieces. **In order to extract copper from an ore it is necessary to take advantage of one of its characteristic properties, its chemical activity.** When an electric current is passed

Figure 17 Ores contain useful amounts of metals that are combined with other elements.
A. Malachite contains copper.
B. Iron pyrite contains iron.
Applying Concepts Why do ores have different properties from the elements that they contain?

through a solution of a copper compound, a chemical change will occur that separates the copper from the other elements in the compound. This process is called electrolysis, which literally means "electric cutting." In **electrolysis,** an electric current breaks the chemical bond that joins the metal and other elements in the compound.

In electrolysis, a battery or other source produces an electric current, which is then carried over wires. At the end of each wire is a metal strip called an **electrode.** The two electrodes are

Isolating Copper

In nature, copper is usually found in compounds with other elements. In this investigation, you will perform an electrolysis to isolate copper from a compound called copper chloride.

Problem

How can pure copper be isolated from a compound by electrolysis?

Skills Focus

observing, inferring

Materials

glass jar, about 250 mL
two paper clips
wires with alligator clips or battery holder with wires
copper chloride solution (0.6 *M*), 50–100 mL

6-volt battery
index card

Procedure

1. Straighten a paper clip into a hook shape. Push the long end through an index card until the hooked part touches the card.

2. Repeat Step 1 with another paper clip so that the clips are about 2–3 cm apart. The paper clips serve as your electrodes.
3. Pour enough copper chloride solution into a jar to cover at least half the length of the paper clips when the index card is set on top of the jar. **CAUTION:** *Copper chloride solution can be irritating to the skin and eyes. Do not touch it with your hands or get it in your mouth. The solution can stain your skin and clothes.*
4. Place the index card on top of the jar. If the straightened ends of the paper clips are not at least half-covered by the copper chloride solution, add more solution.

dipped into a water solution made of the copper ore. When the current is turned on, one electrode attracts the metal in the ore, and the other electrode attracts the other materials.

After the first electrode becomes coated with enough metal atoms, the metal can be scraped off and used. Although electrolysis can occur in a beaker, the copper industry uses electrolysis on a large scale to produce much larger amounts of the metal.

DEVIL In ☆

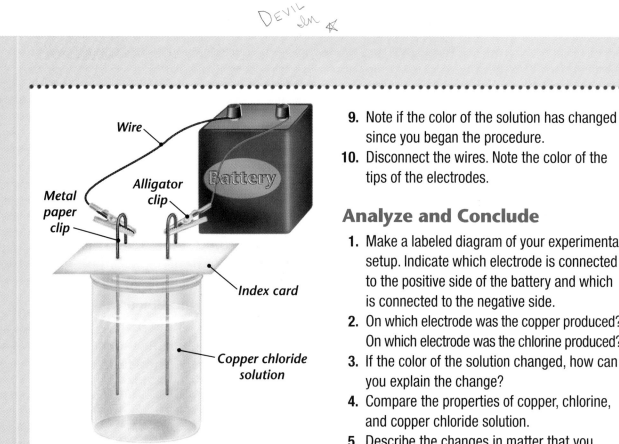

Wire
Alligator clip
Battery
Metal paper clip
Index card
Copper chloride solution

5. Attach a wire to each pole of a battery. Attach the other ends of the wires to a separate paper clip. See the drawing. Prevent the paper clips from touching each other.

6. Predict what you think will happen if you allow the current to run for 2–3 minutes. (*Hint:* What elements are present in the copper chloride solution?)

7. Let the setup run for 2–3 minutes or until you see a deposit forming on one of the electrodes. Also look for bubbles.

8. Remove the index card. Bring your face close to the jar and gently wave your hand toward your nose. Try to detect any odor.

9. Note if the color of the solution has changed since you began the procedure.

10. Disconnect the wires. Note the color of the tips of the electrodes.

Analyze and Conclude

1. Make a labeled diagram of your experimental setup. Indicate which electrode is connected to the positive side of the battery and which is connected to the negative side.

2. On which electrode was the copper produced? On which electrode was the chlorine produced?

3. If the color of the solution changed, how can you explain the change?

4. Compare the properties of copper, chlorine, and copper chloride solution.

5. Describe the changes in matter that you observed. Classify them as physical changes or chemical changes.

6. **Apply** Using your observations of this procedure as evidence, explain why you think copper chloride is a compound, and not a mixture.

More to Explore

Suppose you were to reconnect the wires with the positive and negative sides reversed. Predict how your results would differ under these conditions. With your teacher's permission, carry out the electrolysis with the connections reversed. Was your prediction correct?

Figure 18 It is possible to use large-scale chemical reactions to produce useful material. This blast furnace is used to react carbon with iron ore to produce iron metal. The source of the carbon is coke, a substance produced from coal.

Iron and Chemical Activity

In iron ores, the element iron is also chemically combined with other elements. How can this useful metal be separated from its ores? If chunks of iron-containing ores and a source of carbon are placed into a hot fire, the iron is released.

The key to why this method works lies in the chemical activity of iron ore and carbon. Iron ores most often contain iron combined with oxygen. The carbon comes from a material called coke, which is made from coal. When heated, the carbon reacts with oxygen in the ore, leaving the purified iron metal behind.

Today, you can observe the same purification process in large blast furnaces, such as the one shown in Figure 18. Blast furnaces use huge quantities of coke and very high temperatures to separate iron from crushed iron ore. The purified iron from these furnaces can then be used to make steel, a material in which iron is mixed with other elements.

Section 4 Review

1. Describe how panning for gold takes advantage of one of gold's characteristic properties.
2. How is chemical activity used to separate copper from its ores?
3. What happens to the elements in iron ore when the ore is mixed with carbon and heated?
4. **Thinking Critically Making Judgments** Planet Earth contains a limited supply of all metals. Predict whether programs to recycle aluminum, iron, and other metals will become more important in the future.

Check Your Progress

CHAPTER PROJECT 1

Trade your written procedure and product samples with a new partner. Repeat this partner's procedure, following the directions as exactly as you can. Share your results with your partner. Think of ways to improve both your procedure and your partner's procedure to make them clearer to follow.

SECTION 1 — Describing Matter

Key Ideas

◆ Matter makes up everything in the universe. The three commonly found states of matter are solid, liquid, and gas.

◆ The characteristic properties of a substance can be used to identify the substance.

◆ Physical changes alter the form of a substance, but not its identity. In chemical changes, one or more substances combine or decompose to form new substances.

◆ Matter can be classified into two general categories: mixtures and pure substances. The pure substances include elements and compounds.

Key Terms

characteristic property
boiling point
melting point
physical change
chemical change
chemical activity

mixture
solution
pure substance
element
compound

SECTION 2 — Measuring Matter

Key Ideas

◆ Mass is a measurement of how much matter an object contains. If you move an object away from Earth, its weight changes but its mass stays the same.

◆ The density of an object equals its mass divided by its volume. A unit of density is always a mass unit divided by a volume unit, such as grams per cubic centimeter (g/cm^3).

Key Terms

weight
mass
International System of Units (SI)

volume
density

SECTION 3 — Particles of Matter

Key Ideas

◆ Atoms are extremely small particles from which all elements are made.

◆ Dalton stated that atoms are unbreakable, rigid spheres. He also said that atoms of the same element are exactly alike and that each element is made of its own kind of atoms.

◆ In many cases, the fundamental unit of a compound is a molecule. A molecule is a group of atoms joined together that act as a single unit.

Key Terms

atom
molecule
chemical bond

SECTION 4 — Elements From Earth

INTEGRATING EARTH SCIENCE

Key Ideas

◆ By taking advantage of characteristic properties, it is possible to extract pure elements from their natural forms.

◆ Earth contains deposits of many different metals, usually in combination with other elements. Deposits from which usable amounts of metal can be removed are called ores.

Key Terms

ore
electrolysis
electrode

ACTIVITY

USING THE INTERNET

www.science-explorer.phschool.com

Reviewing Content

For more review of key concepts, see the Interactive Student Tutorial CD-ROM.

Multiple Choice

Choose the letter of the answer that best completes the statement or answers the question.

1. An example of a characteristic property is
   a. size.   b. chemical activity.
   c. amount.   d. shape.
2. The "best mixed" mixtures are called
   a. elements.   b. compounds.
   c. solutions.   d. chemicals.
3. Unlike physical changes, chemical changes always
   a. involve melting or boiling.
   b. form a new substance or new substances.
   c. change the physical state of a substance.
   d. take a relatively long time.
4. The density of an object equals
   a. the product of its length, width, and height.
   b. the volume divided by the mass.
   c. the product of the mass and volume.
   d. the mass divided by the volume.
5. A method used to release iron metal from its ore involves
   a. heating the ore and carbon together.
   b. cooling the ore in an ice bath.
   c. breaking the ore into small pieces.
   d. panning.

True or False

If the statement is true, write true. If it is false, change the underlined word or words to make it true.

6. The temperature at which a pure substance changes from the solid state to the liquid state is called its <u>boiling point</u>.
7. If you move an object from place to place in the universe, the <u>weight</u> of the object will stay the same.
8. Grams per milliliter (g/mL) is an example of a unit of <u>volume</u>.
9. One of Dalton's principles is that each element is made of its own kind of <u>atom</u>.
10. Useful amounts of copper can be isolated during a process called <u>electrolysis</u>.

Checking Concepts

11. When a piece of paper is torn into two pieces, has it undergone a chemical change or a physical change? Explain.
12. How could you find the volume of a small rock, using only a graduated cylinder and water?
13. Why is density considered a characteristic property of a substance, but mass and volume are not?
14. How are atoms related to molecules in a sample of a compound?
15. **Writing to Learn** In a novel or short story, the author describes the properties of objects he or she is writing about. These details add interest to the story. Select at least six different kinds of objects. You might include objects from nature as well as objects made by people. Identify each object by its general and characteristic properties. Now use the descriptions you have developed to write the first paragraph of a story.

Thinking Visually

16. **Concept Map** Copy the concept map about classifying matter onto a separate sheet of paper. Then complete the map and add a title. (For more on concept maps, see the Skills Handbook.)

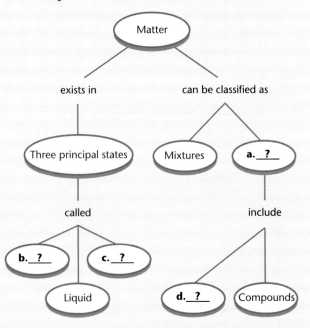

Applying Skills

Use the table below to answer Questions 17–19. The table lists the mass and volume of six coins.

Coin	Mass (g)	Volume (cm^3)
A	3.1	0.41
B	4.0	0.50
C	8.6	1.2
D	8.0	0.95
E	9.8	1.1
F	5.0	0.67

17. **Calculating** Based on the data in the table, calculate the density of Coins A–F.

18. **Interpreting Data** In Altrusia, all coins are made of a mixture of copper and zinc that has a density of 8.42 g/cm^3. Which coins could be from Altrusia?

19. **Drawing Conclusions** The density of copper is 8.92 g/cm^3 and the density of zinc is 7.14 g/cm^3. Which coin, A or B, contains the highest percentage of zinc? Which coin contains the highest percentage of copper? Explain.

Thinking Critically

20. **Comparing and Contrasting** Compare and contrast atoms and molecules. What do the two kinds of particles have in common? How are they related? Give an example that shows this relationship.

21. **Classifying** Which of the following is a solution: cranberry juice, a bowl of cereal and milk, chocolate chip cookie dough?

22. **Problem Solving** How can you show that a solution of salt water is a mixture and not a compound? First compare the properties of the solution to the properties of the individual components. Then come up with a plan to separate the solution into its components.

23. **Applying Concepts** How can you use Dalton's atomic theory to explain why every sample of a pure substance has the same properties?

24. **Inferring** Solid gold has a greater density than liquid gold. What must happen to the volume of a given mass of solid gold when it becomes a liquid? Explain.

Performance Assessment

CHAPTER PROJECT 1 **Wrap Up**

Present Your Project Work with your second partner to show the data each of you collected. The data should be presented so that other students can see whether your procedures produced similar results. Briefly present your procedure and results to the class.

Reflect and Record In your journal, record the results of your experiment and describe any conclusions you reached. Are you satisfied that your conclusions are accurate? If you could repeat the experiment, what improvements would you make to your procedure?

Getting Involved

At Home Make a survey of the matter in your house. Classify the matter as solid, liquid, or gas. Make a table that has each of the three states of matter as column heads. List in each column examples of that state. Which state of matter is most common? Why do you think this is so?

WHAT'S AHEAD

A Story of Changes in Matter

This river is a story of changing matter. In winter, the surface of the river froze solid. Now it's spring, and the ice has begun melting. The ice around each rock is the last to melt. The river water flows downstream, and plants, such as the green moss on the rocks, begin their spring growth.

If you could look very closely at ice, water, rock, and moss, you would be able to see that all matter is made up of small particles. In this chapter, you will learn how the behavior of these small particles explains the properties of solids, liquids, and gases. Your project is to model what happens to particles of matter as they change from a solid to a liquid to a gas.

Your Goal Create a skit or cartoon that demonstrates how particles of matter behave as they change from a solid to a liquid to a gas and then from a gas to a liquid to a solid.

To complete the project, you must
◆ describe what happens to the particles during each change of state
◆ outline your skit or cartoon in a storyboard format
◆ illustrate your cartoon or produce your skit

Get Started With a group of classmates, brainstorm a list of the properties of solids, liquids, and gases.

Check Your Progress You'll be working on this project as you study this chapter. To keep your project on track, look for Check Your Progress boxes at the following points.

Section 2 Review, page 55: Describe the particles in solid, liquid, and gas, and begin preparing a storyboard.
Section 4 Review, page 69: Finish your cartoon or skit.

Wrap Up At the end of the chapter (page 73), you will present your skit or cartoon to the class.

Ice formations on Bridal Veil Creek, Columbia River Gorge National Scenic Area, Oregon

1 Solids, Liquids, and Gases

DISCOVER

ACTIVITY

What Are Solids, Liquids, and Gases?

1. Break an antacid tablet (fizzing type) into three or four pieces. Place them inside a large, uninflated balloon.

2. Fill a 1-liter plastic bottle about halfway with water. Stretch the mouth of the balloon over the top of the bottle, taking care to keep the pieces inside the balloon.

3. Jiggle the balloon so that the pieces fall into the bottle. Observe what happens for about two minutes.

4. Remove the balloon and examine its contents.

Think It Over

Forming Operational Definitions Identify examples of the different states of matter—solids, liquids, and gases—that you observed in this activity. Define each of the three states in your own words.

GUIDE FOR READING

◆ How are shape, volume, and particle motion useful in describing solids, liquids, and gases?

Reading Tip Before you read, list properties that you think characterize solids, liquids, and gases. Revise your list as you read.

If you visit the annual Winter Carnival in St. Paul, Minnesota, you will see some unusual structures. To celebrate the cold winter weather, people carve huge sculptures out of ice. Over the years, the carnival has featured giant snowmen and ice palaces like the one shown here.

Even in Minnesota, anything made of snow and ice won't last beyond winter. When the temperature rises, snowmen and ice palaces melt into liquid water. And unlike frozen water, liquid water is a poor building material.

Your world is full of substances that can be classified as solids, liquids, or gases. Water is, of course, a common liquid. Although it's easy to list examples of the three states of matter, defining them is more difficult. To define solids, liquids, and gases, you need to examine their properties. As you will see, the states of matter are defined mainly by whether or not they hold their volume and shape.

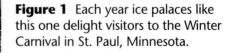

Figure 1 Each year ice palaces like this one delight visitors to the Winter Carnival in St. Paul, Minnesota.

Figure 2 In the tanks on their backs these scuba divers carry air to breathe. *Classifying Find an example of each state of matter in this photograph.*

Solids

What if you were to pick up a solid object, such as a pen or a comb, and move it from place to place around the room? What would you observe? Would the object ever change its size or shape as you moved it? Would a pen become larger if you put it in a bowl? Would a comb become flatter when you place it on a tabletop? Of course not. A **solid** has a definite volume and a definite shape. If your pen has a volume of 6 cm^3 and a cylindrical shape, then it will keep that volume and shape in any position and in any container.

Particles in a Solid The particles that make up a solid are packed very closely together, as shown in Figure 3A. In addition, each particle is tightly fixed in one position. This makes it hard to separate them. **Because the particles in a solid are packed tightly together and stay in fixed positions, a solid has a definite shape and volume.**

Are the particles in a solid completely motionless? No, not really. The particles vibrate, meaning they move back and forth slightly. This motion is similar to a person running in place. You can think of the particles in a solid as something like a group of balls connected by tight springs. Like the balls in Figure 3B, the particles that make up a solid stay in about the same position. However, the individual pieces are still able to vibrate back and forth in their places.

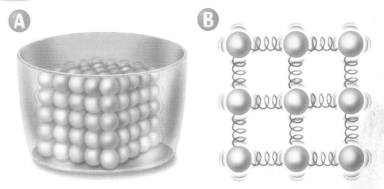

Figure 3 The blue balls represent the particles in a solid. **A.** A solid keeps its own shape. It doesn't take the shape of a container. **B.** The particles vibrate back and forth within the solid.

Figure 4 When you heat an amorphous solid such as this butter, it softens before it melts.

Types of Solids In many solids, the particles form a regular, repeating pattern. These patterns create crystals. Solids that are made up of crystals are called **crystalline solids** (KRIS tuh lin). Salt, sugar, sand, and snow are examples of crystalline solids. When a crystalline solid such as snow is heated, it melts at a distinct, characteristic melting point.

In other solids the particles are not arranged in a regular pattern. These solids are called **amorphous solids** (uh MAWR fus). Plastics, rubber, and glass are amorphous solids. Unlike a crystalline solid, an amorphous solid does not have a distinct melting point. Instead, when it is heated it becomes softer and softer as its temperature rises. You have probably noticed this property in plastic items that have been out in the sun on a hot day. The plastic gradually melts. In fact, the word *plastic* means "able to be molded into many shapes."

✓ *Checkpoint* How do crystalline and amorphous solids differ?

Liquids

Unlike a solid, a **liquid** has no shape of its own. Instead, a liquid takes on the shape of its container. Without a container, a liquid spreads into a wide, shallow puddle.

However, liquids are like solids in that they do not easily compress or expand. If you tried to squeeze water between your palms, for example, the water might change its shape, but its volume would not decrease or increase.

What if you have 100 mL of water? If you pour it into another container, the water still fills 100 mL. It has the same volume no matter the shape of the container.

Figure 5 Although a liquid's volume does not change, it takes the shape of whatever container you pour it into. *Comparing and Contrasting How do the particles of a liquid differ from the particles of a solid?*

Figure 6 You can think of the particles of a liquid as somewhat like the people in this train station. Both the liquid and the crowd can flow.

Particles in a Liquid The particles in a liquid are packed almost as closely as in a solid. However, the particles in a liquid move around each other freely. **Because its particles are free to move, a liquid has no definite shape. However, it does have a definite volume.** You can compare a liquid to the crowd at a train station. Like particles in a liquid, the people in the crowd move around the room that contains them, but they stay in close contact with each other.

Viscosity Because particles in a liquid are free to move around each other, a liquid can flow from place to place. For this reason, a liquid is also called a **fluid**—meaning "a substance that flows."

Some liquids flow more easily than others. The resistance of a liquid to flowing is called **viscosity** (vis KAHS uh tee). Liquids with high viscosity flow slowly. Cold molasses is an example of a liquid with a particularly high viscosity. Liquids with low viscosity flow quickly. Water has relatively low viscosity.

 INTEGRATING EARTH SCIENCE The viscosity of lava that erupts from a volcano helps determine the type of volcanic eruption. A volcano erupts quietly if it has thin, runny lava—that is, lava with low viscosity. High-viscosity lava, which is thick and sticky, is typical of a volcano that erupts explosively.

Gases

Unlike solids and liquids, a **gas** can change volume very easily. If you put a gas in a container with a top, the gas will spread apart or squeeze together to fill that container. The volume and shape of a gas is the volume and shape of its container. To illustrate this principle, take a deep breath. Your chest expands. Can you feel

As Thick as Honey

Here's how you can compare the viscosity of two liquids.

1. Place on a table a clear plastic jar almost filled with honey and another clear plastic jar almost filled with vegetable oil. Make sure that the tops of both jars are tightly closed.

2. Turn the jars upside down at the same time. Observe what happens.

3. Turn the two jars right-side up and again watch what happens.

Observing Which fluid has a greater viscosity? What evidence leads you to this conclusion?

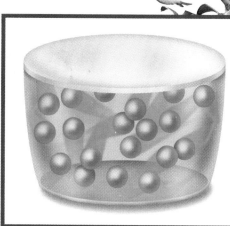

Figure 7 The particles of a gas can be squeezed into a small volume. If allowed to, they will spread out without limit, somewhat like this flock of gulls.

the air coming through your nose and mouth? Air is a mixture of gases that acts as one gas. When you breathe in, air moves from your mouth to your windpipe to your lungs. In each place, the air changes shape and volume. When you breathe out, the changes happen in reverse. If you hold your hand in front of your mouth, you can feel the air move around and past your fingers.

If you could see the individual particles that make up a gas, you would see tiny particles flying at high speeds in all directions. **Gas particles spread apart, filling all the space available to them. Thus, a gas has neither definite shape nor volume.** You can compare a gas to the flock of gulls shown in Figure 7. Like gas particles, these gulls fly very quickly in different directions. They can spread out to "fill" any available space or they can all cluster together.

Section 1 Review

1. Describe how particles in a solid are arranged.
2. How does the movement of particles in a liquid help to explain the shape and volume of liquids?
3. Use what you know about the particles in a gas to explain why a gas has no definite shape and no definite volume.
4. **Thinking Critically Relating Cause and Effect** Glass is an amorphous solid. How can you use that information to help explain why a glassblower can bend and shape a piece of glass that has been heated?

Science at Home

Show your family how liquids and gases differ. Fill the bulb and cylinder of a turkey baster with water. Try to get it as full as possible. Seal the end with your finger and hold it over the sink. Have a family member squeeze the bulb. Now empty the turkey baster. Again, seal the end with your finger and have a family member squeeze the bulb. Did the person notice any difference? Use what you know about the particles in liquids and gases to explain your observations.

2 Behavior of Gases

DISCOVER • ACTIVITY

How Can Air Keep Chalk From Breaking?

1. Standing on a chair or table, drop a piece of chalk onto a hard floor. Observe what happens to the chalk.

2. Wrap a second piece of chalk in wax paper or plastic food wrap. Drop the chalk from the same height used in Step 1. Observe the results.

3. Wrap a third piece of chalk in plastic bubble wrap. Drop the chalk from the same height used in Step 1. Observe the results.

Think It Over

Inferring Compare the results from Steps 1, 2, and 3. What properties of the air in the bubble wrap accounted for the results in Step 3?

Every Thanksgiving, the people of New York City gather to watch a big parade. Maybe you have seen this parade on television, or even in person. The parade is famous for its large, floating balloons, like the one shown on this page. The balloons float because they are filled with helium, a gas that is less dense than air.

If you were in charge of a parade balloon, you would be faced with many different questions. How large should the balloon be? How much helium should you put inside the balloon? Does the balloon behave differently in warm weather than in cold weather? To answer these questions and others like them, you would need to understand the properties of gases.

GUIDE FOR READING

◆ How are the volume, temperature, and pressure of a gas related?

Reading Tip Before you read, change each heading into a question. Write a brief answer to each question as you read.

Figure 8 A helium balloon of Clifford, the Big Red Dog, floats past Central Park in New York City.

Figure 9 The helium gas in this tank is kept under high pressure within the volume set by the thick steel walls. *Predicting What will happen to the helium atoms when the entire contents of the tank has been used to fill balloons?*

Measuring Gases

How much helium is in the tank in Figure 9? You may think that measuring the volume of the tank will give you an answer. But gases easily squeeze together or spread out. To fill the tank, helium was compressed, or pressed together tightly. When the helium is used, it fills a total volume of inflated balloons much greater than the volume of the tank. The actual volume you get, however, depends on the temperature and air pressure that day. So what exactly do measurements of volume, pressure, and temperature mean?

Volume You know volume is the amount of space that matter fills. Volume is measured in cubic centimeters, milliliters, liters, and other units. Because gases fill the space available, the volume of a gas is the same as the volume of its container.

Temperature Hot soup, warm hands, cool breezes—you should be familiar with matter at different temperatures. But what exactly does temperature measure? Recall that in any substance—solid, liquid, or gas—the particles are constantly moving. Temperature is a measure of the average energy of motion of the particles of a substance. The faster the particles are moving, the greater their energy and the higher the temperature. You might think of a thermometer as a speedometer for molecules.

Even at ordinary temperatures, the average speed of particles in a gas is very fast. At 20°C, which is about room temperature, the particles in a typical gas travel about 500 meters per second!

Pressure Because gas particles are moving, they constantly collide with one another. They also collide with the walls of their container. As a result, the gas exerts an outward push on the walls of the container. The **pressure** of the gas is the force of its outward push divided by the area of the walls of the container. Pressure is measured in units of kilopascals (kPa).

$$Pressure = \frac{Force}{Area}$$

The firmness of an object inflated with a gas, such as a soccer ball, comes from the pressure of the gas. If the gas (in this case, air) leaks out of the ball, the pressure decreases and the ball becomes softer. But why does a ball leak when punctured? A gas flows from an area of high pressure to an area of low pressure. The air inside the ball is at higher pressure than the air outside. Gas particles inside the ball hit the hole with tremendous force and fly out. Gas particles outside also hit the hole. But since fewer outside particles hit the hole, they have less chance of getting in through the hole. Thus, many more particles go out than in. The pressure inside drops until it is equal to the pressure outside.

Checkpoint *What are three properties of a gas that you can measure?*

Relating Pressure and Volume

Pressure is also related to the volume of a container. For example, imagine that you are operating a bicycle pump. By pressing down on the plunger, you force the gas inside the pump through the rubber tube and out the nozzle into the tire. What will happen if you push the plunger halfway down and close the nozzle? As you

Figure 10 The gas particles are in constant motion, colliding with each other and with the walls of their container.

Figure 11 What will happen when this bicyclist operates the pump she is attaching? She will decrease the volume of air in the cylinder and increase its pressure. As a result, air will be forced into the bicycle tire and the tire will inflate.

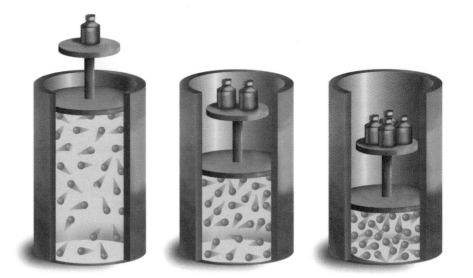

Figure 12 As weights are added on top, the same number of particles occupies a smaller volume. The pressure of the gas increases. This relationship is called Boyle's law.

Balloon Test

ACTIVITY

What happens when you change the volume of a gas?

1. Hold the open end of a paper cup on the side of a partially inflated balloon.

2. Inflate the balloon until it presses against the cup and then let go of the cup. What happens?

Developing Hypotheses Use what you know about pressure and volume to write a hypothesis that explains the behavior of the cup after you let it go. How could you test your hypothesis?

continue to push on the plunger, the volume of the air trapped inside the pump will get smaller and its pressure will increase.

The pressure and volume of a gas behave in a predictable way. The relationship between the pressure and volume of a gas at constant temperature is named **Boyle's law,** after the English scientist Robert Boyle. In the 1600s, Boyle measured the volumes of gases at different pressures as he experimented with ways to improve air pumps. **According to Boyle's law, when the pressure of a gas increases, its volume decreases. When the pressure of a gas decreases, its volume increases.** Likewise, when the volume of a gas changes, its pressure changes the opposite way.

You can observe Boyle's law with a simple experiment. Squeeze an air-filled object, such as a balloon. When you squeeze the balloon, you are decreasing its volume slightly. You should be able to feel the increasing pressure of the gas inside it.

INTEGRATING EARTH SCIENCE Boyle's law plays an important role in research done with some high-altitude balloons. These balloons are made from lightweight plastic. They are filled with only a small fraction of the helium they could hold. Why is that? As a balloon rises through the atmosphere, the air pressure around it decreases steadily. As the air pressure decreases, the helium inside the balloon expands, stretching the balloon to a greater and greater volume. If the balloon were fully filled at takeoff, it would burst from the change in air pressure long before it got very high.

✓ *Checkpoint* *What is Boyle's law?*

Relating Pressure and Temperature

If you drop a few grains of sand onto your skin, they will not hurt at all. But suppose you are caught in a sandstorm. Because the sand grains are flying very fast, they will hurt a great deal! The faster the grains are traveling, the harder they will hit your skin.

Raising Temperature Raises Pressure

Although gas particles are much smaller and lighter than sand grains, a sandstorm is a good model for a gas. Like sand in a sandstorm, gas particles travel individually and at high speeds. Remember that pressure is a measure of how much gas particles push on the walls of a container. The greater the speed of the gas particles, the more collisions will occur. The more collisions there are, the greater the pressure will be.

Temperature is a measure of the speed of the particles of a gas. The higher the temperature of a gas, the faster the gas particles move. So now you have a relationship between temperature and pressure. **When the temperature of a gas increases, its pressure increases. When the temperature of a gas decreases, its pressure decreases.** This relationship applies to a gas that cannot change its volume, such as a gas kept in a closed, rigid container.

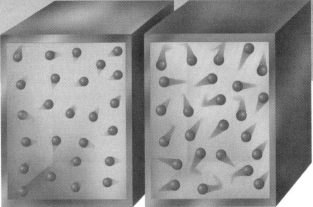

Figure 13 Particles of a gas are like the sand blown by the wind in this sandstorm. When a gas is heated, the particles move faster and collide more with each other and the sides of their container. *Relating Cause and Effect Which container shows a gas at a higher temperature? How can you tell?*

Pressure and Temperature in Action Have you ever looked at the tires of an 18-wheel truck? Because these tires need to support a lot of weight, they are large, heavy, and stiff. The inside volume of these tires doesn't vary much.

On long trips, especially in the summer, a truck's tires can get very hot. As the temperature increases, so does the pressure of the air inside the tire. If the pressure becomes higher than the tire can hold, the tire will burst apart. For this reason, truck drivers need to monitor and adjust tire pressure on long trips.

Relating Volume and Temperature

If the temperature of the gas in a balloon is increased, its volume will change. Will the volume increase or decrease? If you answered "increase," you are right. Most substances increase in size when their temperature increases. As their temperature decreases, they become smaller. People in charge of the large balloons used for parades need to understand the effect temperature has on volume so that the balloons can be inflated properly. The same principle applies to the smaller balloons at a party.

Charles's Law   In the late 1700s, a French scientist named Jacques Charles examined the relationship between the temperature and volume of a gas kept at a constant pressure. He measured the volume of a gas at various temperatures in a container whose volume could change. **Charles found that when the temperature of a gas increases, its volume increases.** This principle is called **Charles's law.** Remember that at higher temperatures, the particles move faster. As a result, they collide more often with the walls around them. As long as the volume of the container can change, the total push of the collisions results in the gas taking up more space. The volume of the gas increases. Similarly, if the temperature of a gas decreases, then its volume decreases.

Charles's Law in Action   Picture a basketball game with a player dribbling the ball down the floor of the gym past the opposing team. Each time she dribbles the ball, it responds with a lively bounce. Then, when the game is over, she takes the ball home but leaves it outside her front door. Overnight the temperature drops to –4°C.

Figure 14 If the temperature is increased, the same number of particles of gas will occupy a greater volume. This relationship is called Charles's law.

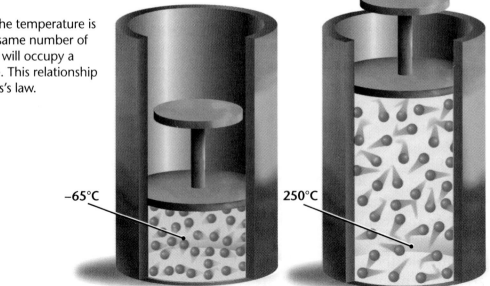

–65°C

250°C

Figure 15 It is 26°C inside the gym where this basketball game is being played. Outside it is only –4°C. *Predicting How might the basketball change if it were left outside in the playground?*

The next morning, the player picks up the ball and decides to shoot a couple of baskets in the playground outside. Again, she starts to dribble the ball. When the ball hits the ground—splat— it just stays there! Why did the ball become soft since the game the night before? A basketball is inflated with air, but no air leaked out of the ball. You can use Charles's law to explain. The ball lost its bounce because the volume of the air inside decreased, chilled by the cold winter air. The same amount of a gas occupies a smaller volume at a lower temperature. Can the ball recover its bounce? Yes, the ball will return to its full volume in the warmth of the school gym.

Section 2 Review

1. Describe the relationship between the pressure and volume of a gas.
2. If you change the temperature of a gas but keep the volume the same, how does the pressure change?
3. What is Charles's law?
4. **Thinking Critically Applying Concepts** Suppose it is the night before Thanksgiving, and you are in charge of inflating a balloon for the Thanksgiving Day parade. You just learned that the temperature will rise 15°C by the time the parade starts. How should you change the way you inflate your balloon?

Check Your Progress

CHAPTER
PROJECT
2

With the members of your group, write a description of how particles behave in each of the three states of matter. Next, think of different ways to model each state, using drawings and words. Decide if you want to demonstrate a change of state as cartoon pictures or by acting out the motion of particles in a skit. (*Hint:* Prepare a storyboard. A storyboard is a series of simple drawings and captions that outline the action of a story.)

SECTION 3 Graphing Gas Behavior

DISCOVER ● **ACTIVITY**

What Does a Graph of Pressure and Temperature Show?

Temperature (°C)	Pressure (kPa)
0	8
5	11
10	14
15	17
20	20
25	23

1. In an experiment, the temperature was varied for a constant volume of gas. Gas pressure was measured after each 5°C change. You now need to graph the data in this table.

2. Show temperature on the horizontal axis with a scale from 0°C to 25°C. Show pressure on the vertical axis with a scale equally spaced from 0 kPa to 25 kPa.

3. For each pair of measurements, draw a point on the graph.

4. Draw a line to connect the points.

Think It Over

Graphing Use the graph to describe the relationship between the pressure and temperature of a gas.

GUIDE FOR READING

◆ What do graphs for Charles's law and Boyle's law look like?

Reading Tip As you read about the experiments in this section, refer to the graphs in Figures 19 and 21.

The population of a town is increasing. The schools are becoming more crowded, and the people need to decide whether to build more schools. Newspapers illustrate their articles about the problem with graphs.

How could a graph help tell this story? **Graphs** are diagrams that tell how two variables are related. Graphs show how changes in one variable result in changes in a second variable. You can use graphs to make predictions. For example, according to the graph in Figure 16, the town might have a population of 32,000 in 2020. That assumes, of course, that population continues to grow at the same rate. In this section, you will learn how to interpret graphs that relate properties of gases.

Figure 16 This graph shows that population in the town is growing steadily. The dashed line predicts what the population would be if the current growth rate continues.

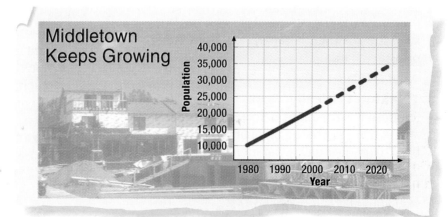

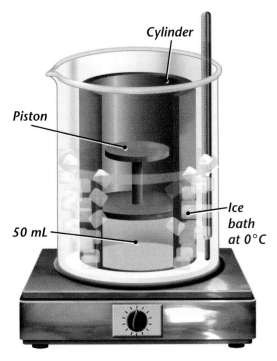

Cylinder

Piston

50 mL

Ice bath at 0°C

Temperature		Volume
(°C)	(K)	(mL)
0	273	50
10	283	52
20	293	54
30	303	56
40	313	58
50	323	60
60	333	62
70	343	63
80	353	66
90	363	67
100	373	69

Figure 17 As the temperature of the water bath increases, the gas inside the cylinder is warmed by the water. The data from the experiment are recorded in the table. Celsius temperature measurements are converted to kelvins by adding 273 to each value.

Temperature and Volume

Recall from Section 2 that Charles's law relates the temperature and volume of a gas kept at a constant pressure. You can examine this relationship by doing an experiment in which you change the temperature of a gas and measure its volume. Then you can graph the data you have recorded and look for a relationship.

Collecting Data As you can see from the cutaway view in Figure 17, the gas in the experiment is in a cylinder that has a movable piston. The piston moves up and down freely, which allows the gas to change volume and keep the same pressure. To control the temperature of the gas, the cylinder is placed in a water bath.

The experiment begins with an ice-water bath at 0°C, and the gas volume at 50 mL. Then the water bath is slowly heated. Very gradually, the temperature increases from 0°C to 100°C. Each time the temperature increases by 10°C, the volume of the gas in the cylinder is recorded.

You'll notice a second set of temperatures listed in the table. Scientists often work with gas temperatures in units called kelvins. To convert from Celsius degrees to kelvins, you add 273. The kelvin temperatures will be used to graph the data.

Graphing the Results A graph consists of a grid set up by two lines—one horizontal and one vertical. Each line, or axis, is divided into equal units. The horizontal, or *x*-, axis shows the manipulated variable. The vertical, or *y*-, axis shows the

Figure 18 The horizontal, or *x*-, axis and the vertical, or *y*-, axis are the "backbone" of a graph.

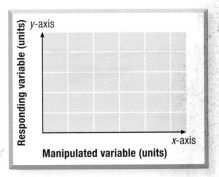

y-axis

Responding variable (units)

Manipulated variable (units)

x-axis

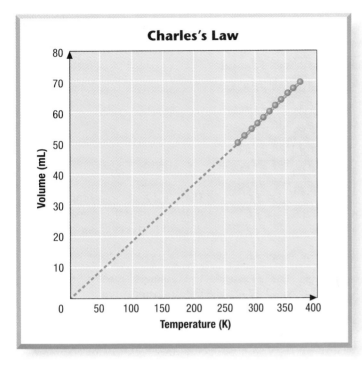

Charles's Law

[Graph: x-axis labeled "Temperature (K)" ranging 0 to 400; y-axis labeled "Volume (mL)" ranging 0 to 80. A dotted line rises from near the origin through plotted data points between about 270 K and 380 K.]

Figure 19 This graph of the data from Figure 17 shows the relationship between temperature and volume known as Charles's law. The dotted line predicts how the graph would look if the gas could be cooled to lower temperatures.

responding variable. Each axis is labeled with a range of units for the appropriate variable. In this case, kelvins are on the *x*-axis and milliliters are on the *y*-axis.

Look at the graph in Figure 19. It appears as if the line would continue downward if data could be collected for lower temperatures. Such a line would pass through the point (0, 0). When a graph of two variables is a straight line passing through the (0, 0) point, the variables are said to be **directly proportional** to each other. **The graph of Charles's law shows that the volume of a gas is directly proportional to its kelvin temperature under constant pressure.**

☑ *Checkpoint* *On which axis of a graph do you show the responding variable?*

Pressure and Volume

You can perform another experiment to show how pressure and volume are related when temperature is kept constant. Recall that the relationship between pressure and volume is called Boyle's law.

Figure 20 By pushing on the top of the piston, you compress the gas and thereby increase the pressure of the gas inside the cylinder. The data from the experiment are recorded in the table.
Predicting What would happen if you pulled up on the piston?

Volume (mL)	Pressure (kPa)
100	60
90	67
80	75
70	86
60	100

Collecting Data The gas in this experiment is also contained in a cylinder with a movable piston. In this case, however, a pressure gauge indicates the pressure of the gas inside.

The experiment begins with the volume of the gas at 100 mL. The pressure of the gas is 60 kilopascals. Next, the piston is slowly pushed into the cylinder, compressing the gas, or shrinking its volume. The pressure of the gas is recorded after each 10-mL change in volume.

Graphing the Results To observe the relationship of the pressure and volume of a gas, it helps to display the data in another graph. In the pressure–volume experiment, the manipulated variable is volume. Volume is shown on the scale of the horizontal axis from 60 mL to 100 mL. The responding variable is pressure. Pressure is shown on the scale of the vertical axis from 60 kPa to 100 kPa.

As you can see in Figure 21, the points lie on a curve. Notice that the curve slopes downward from left to right. Also notice that the curve is steep close to the vertical axis and becomes less steep close to the horizontal axis. When a graph of two measurements forms this kind of curve, the measurements are said to **vary inversely** with one another. **The graph for Boyle's law shows that the pressure of a gas varies inversely with its volume at constant temperature.** In other words, the pressure of a gas decreases as its volume increases.

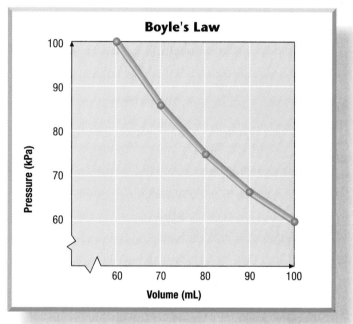

Figure 21 This graph of the data from Figure 20 shows the relationship between pressure and volume known as Boyle's law. (The broken lines between 0 and 60 show gaps in the scales.)

Section 3 Review

1. Describe a graph of Charles's law.
2. Describe a graph of Boyle's law.
3. How can you tell the difference between a graph in which one variable is directly proportional to another and a graph in which two variables vary inversely?
4. **Thinking Critically** **Interpreting Graphs** In the experiment illustrated in Figure 17, the temperature of the gas was increased to 400 K (127°C). Use Figure 19 to predict the volume of the gas at this temperature.

Science at Home

Look for graphs in your newspaper or in news magazines. Point out to members of your family which variable is the manipulated variable and which is the responding variable for each graph. Then compare any line graphs you have found to the graphs in this section. Which of your graphs show two variables that are directly proportional to each other? Do any show variables that vary inversely?

It's a gas

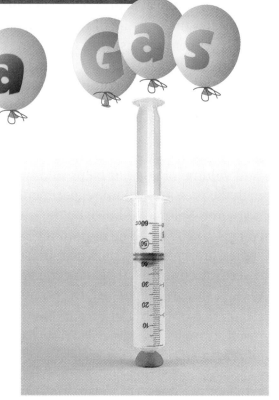

You can use a syringe as a model of an air pump. In this lab, you will determine how the amount you press on a syringe is related to the volume of the air inside it.

Problem

How does the volume of a gas change as the pressure you exert on it increases?

Materials

strong plastic syringe (with no needle), at least 35 cm^3 capacity
modeling clay
4 books of uniform weight

Procedure

1. Make a data table in your notebook like the one below.
2. Lift the plunger of the syringe as high as it will move without going off scale. The volume inside the syringe will then be as large as possible.
3. Seal the small opening of the syringe with a piece of clay. The seal must be airtight.

4. Hold the syringe upright with the clay end on the table. With the help of a partner, place a single book on top of the plunger. Balance the book carefully so it does not fall.
5. Read the volume indicated by the plunger and record it in your data table.
6. Predict what will happen as more books are placed on the syringe.
7. Place another book on top of the first book. Read the new volume and record it in your data table.

DATA TABLE

Adding Books		Removing Books	
Number of Books	Volume (cm^3)	Number of Books	Volume (cm^3)
0		4	
1		3	
2		2	
3		1	
4		0	

8. One by one, place each of the remaining books on top of the plunger. After you add each book, record the volume of the syringe in your data table.

9. Predict what will happen as books are removed from the plunger one by one.

10. Remove the books one at a time. After you remove each book, again record the volume of the syringe in your data table.

Analyze and Conclude

1. Make a line graph of the data obtained from Steps 5, 7, and 8. Show volume in cubic centimeters (cm^3) on the vertical axis and number of books on the horizontal axis. Title this Graph 1.

2. Make a second line graph of the data obtained from Step 10. Title this Graph 2.

3. Did the results you obtained support your predictions in Steps 6 and 9? Explain.

4. Describe the shape of Graph 1. What does the graph tell you about the relationship between the volume and pressure of a gas?

5. Compare Graph 2 with Graph 1. How can you explain any differences in the two graphs?

6. **Think About It** Did the volume change between the addition of the first and second book? Did it change by the same amount between the addition of the second book and third book? Between the third and fourth book? What is happening to the gas particles in air that could explain this behavior?

Design an Experiment

How could you use ice and warm water to show how the temperature and volume of a gas are related? Design an experiment to test the effect of changing the temperature of a gas. With your teacher's approval, conduct this experiment.

DISCOVER ·· ACTIVITY

How Does a Burning Candle Differ From Boiling Water?

1. Put on your goggles.

2. Place a small beaker half-filled with water on a hot plate. Turn the hot plate to a medium-high setting so that the water will boil.

3. Add about half a cup of cold water to an empty soda can.

4. 🔥 Use modeling clay to stand a candle in a small aluminum pie pan. Light the candle.

5. 🔧 Use tongs to hold the can about 3 cm over the candle for about a minute.

6. Move the soda can away from the candle. When the soda can has cooled, examine its bottom side.

7. Blow out the candle. Repeat Steps 3, 5, and 6 with a different soda can, but hold the can over the boiling water.

Think It Over

Posing Questions Compare the substances that collected on the bottom of each soda can. Identify any changes in matter that you observed. What questions would you need to ask to determine whether each change was physical or chemical?

GUIDE FOR READING

◆ How do physical and chemical changes differ?

◆ How do energy changes affect matter?

◆ What is a change of state?

Reading Tip As you read, compare and contrast the various physical and chemical changes.

Your world depends on changing matter. Water changes from a liquid to solid ice in a freezer. Plants change raw materials from air and soil into stems and leaves. Cars and buses burn gasoline to move from place to place. If you look around, you can find lots of examples of substances changing shape, form, or identity.

Energy and Change

As you know, there are two kinds of changes in matter: physical changes and chemical changes. Some examples of physical change include tearing a piece of paper, bending a nail, or spinning wool into yarn. **A physical change alters the form of a substance, but does not change it to another substance.**

Matter can also change by means of a chemical change. Burning wood is a good example. **When a substance undergoes a chemical change, it is changed into a different substance with different properties.** The wood is changed into completely different substances, such as carbon dioxide gas and solid ash.

Figure 22 A jeweler melts silver before pouring it into a mold. The glow stick gives off a greenish glow. *Classifying Which of these examples is most likely a physical change? Which example may be a chemical change?*

INTEGRATING PHYSICS To explain changes in matter, scientists talk about the effects of energy. It's not easy to define "energy." You can give examples: Light and motion are two types of energy. Every substance also contains energy from the movement of its particles, called **thermal energy.** The higher the temperature of a substance, the greater its thermal energy. Another form of energy comes from the chemical bonds within matter. This form of energy is called **chemical energy.**

Any substance can either gain energy or lose energy. In either case, the substance changes in some way. **Matter changes whenever energy is added or taken away.** When something is heated, it gains thermal energy. When something cools, it loses thermal energy to its surroundings. Many physical and chemical changes involve heating or cooling. In order for pancakes to brown on a griddle, the chemical changes require heating. When a mixture of milk, cream, sugar, and flavors becomes ice cream, the physical change requires cooling.

In every physical change and chemical change, the total amount of energy stays the same, a principle which is called the **law of conservation of energy.** The word *conservation* comes from *conserve,* which means "to protect from loss." Energy can change from one form to another, but energy can never be lost.

For example, an unlit match contains chemical energy. When the match is lit, the chemical energy changes into light energy and thermal energy. The total amount of energy produced is equal to the amount of chemical energy in the unlit match. No energy is lost. It only changes from one form to another.

✓ *Checkpoint* What is chemical energy?

Changes Between Liquid and Solid

Remember that the common states of matter are solid, liquid, and gas. **Under certain conditions, a substance can change from any one state of matter to any other.**

Melting The change in state from a solid to a liquid is **melting**. In most pure substances, melting occurs at a specific temperature, called the melting point. The melting point of a substance depends on how strongly its particles attract one another.

Think of a melting ice cube. The energy to melt comes from the air in the room. At first, the added thermal energy makes the water molecules vibrate faster, which raises their temperature.

Eventually, when the temperature of the ice reaches 0°C, the water molecules are vibrating so fast that they break free from their positions in ice crystals. When this happens, the temperature of the ice stops increasing. Instead, the added energy changes the arrangement of the water molecules from ice crystals into liquid water. This is the process you observe as melting.

Freezing Now suppose you put the liquid water from the melted ice cube into a freezer. After an hour or so, the water will freeze back into ice. **Freezing** is the change of state from liquid to solid—just the reverse of melting.

When you put liquid water into the freezer compartment of a refrigerator, the water loses energy to the cold air in the freezer. At first, the water molecules move more slowly. This means that the temperature of the water drops. When the temperature reaches 0°C, the molecules are moving so slowly that they form regular patterns. These patterns are the crystals that form ice.

When water freezes, the temperature stays at 0°C until freezing is complete. (This is the same temperature at which ice melts.) The energy loss during freezing changes the arrangement of the molecules, from liquid water into ice crystals.

Social Studies
CONNECTION

In the United States, home refrigerators became common in the 1920s. Before then, people relied on ice to keep food cold. In the winter, blocks of ice were cut from frozen lakes, as in the photo below, and stored in buildings called ice houses. Many people earned their livings by supplying ice to homes and businesses.

In Your Journal

Imagine the time is about 80 years ago. For years, your family has earned a comfortable living in the ice business. You have just heard about a new product called a refrigerator. Write a letter in which you describe your opinions of this product. How will it change your life?

Figure 23 In this photo taken in New England about 1890, you can see the pond ice was cut into large blocks. The blocks were stored in the icehouse.

Changes Between Liquid and Gas

For other examples of matter changing state, look up at the sky. Have you ever wondered how clouds form, or why rain falls from clouds? And after a rain shower, why do puddles dry up in the sunshine? To answer each of these questions, you need to look at the ways that water changes between the liquid and gas states.

Vaporization Liquid water changing into water vapor is an example of **vaporization** (vay puhr ih ZAY shuhn). Vaporization occurs when a liquid gains enough energy to become a gas.

There are two main types of vaporization. When vaporization takes place only on the surface of the liquid, the process is called **evaporation** (ee vap uh RAY shuhn). A puddle drying up after a rain shower is one example of evaporation. As the water in the puddle gains energy from the ground, the air, or the sun, the molecules on the surface of the puddle gradually escape into the atmosphere. You also can observe evaporation whenever you sweat. Beads of sweat evaporate into the air as they gain energy from your skin. Because your skin is losing energy, sweating helps keep you cool on a hot day or when you exercise.

When vaporization takes place inside a liquid as well as at the surface, the process is called **boiling.** Each liquid boils only at a certain temperature. That temperature is called its boiling point. Like the melting point of a solid, the boiling point of a liquid depends on how strongly the particles attract one other.

Boiling Point and Air Pressure Boiling point also depends

![Integrating Earth Science icon] **INTEGRATING EARTH SCIENCE** on the pressure of the air above a liquid. The lower the air pressure above the liquid, the less energy that liquid molecules need to escape into the air. As you go up in elevation, air pressure decreases. At the air pressure in places close to sea level, the boiling point of water is 100°C. In the mountains, however, air pressure is lower and so is the boiling point of water.

Figure 24 Water evaporates from the surface of a wet road. *Making Generalizations What happens to water molecules when they evaporate?*

Figure 25 A pot on the stove boils when water inside reaches its boiling point.

Figure 26 The water vapor in your warm breath condenses on the cool surface of the mirror. *Classifying What state of matter is the condensation on the glass?*

For example, the city of Denver, Colorado, is 1,600 meters above sea level. At this elevation, the boiling point of water is 95°C. Cooks in Denver have to be careful when a recipe calls for boiling water. Food doesn't cook as quickly at 95°C as it does at 100°C.

Condensation The opposite of vaporization is called condensation. **Condensation** occurs when a gas loses enough thermal energy to become a liquid. Clouds typically form when water vapor in the atmosphere condenses into liquid droplets. When the droplets get heavy enough, they fall to the ground as rain.

You can observe condensation by breathing onto a mirror. When warm water vapor in your breath reaches the cooler surface of the mirror, the water vapor condenses into liquid droplets. The droplets then evaporate into water vapor again.

When you observe vaporization and condensation, remember that you cannot see water vapor. Water vapor is a clear gas, and is impossible to see. The steam you see above a boiling kettle is not water vapor, and neither are clouds or fog. Instead, what you see in each of them is tiny droplets of liquid water suspended in the air.

☑ *Checkpoint* *How are vaporization and condensation related but different?*

Figure 27 Dry ice is solid carbon dioxide. It changes directly to gaseous carbon dioxide in the process of sublimation. The energy absorbed in this change of state cools the water vapor in the air, creating fog.

Changes Between Solid and Gas

If you live where the winters are cold, you may have noticed that snow seems to disappear even if the temperature stays well below freezing. This happens because of a process called sublimation. **Sublimation** occurs when the surface particles of a solid gain enough energy to become a gas. Particles do not pass through the liquid state at all.

One example of sublimation is the change that dry ice undergoes. Dry ice is the common name for solid carbon dioxide. At ordinary pressures, carbon dioxide cannot exist as a liquid. Instead of melting, solid carbon dioxide changes directly into a gas. Dry ice takes in thermal energy as it changes state, which keeps materials near it cold and dry. For this reason, dry ice is an excellent way to keep temperatures low when a refrigerator is not available. When dry ice becomes a gas, it cools water vapor in the nearby air. As a result, fog forms.

EXPLORING Changes of State

What changes occur as you slowly heat a beaker of ice from –10°C to 110°C?

A Solid
Below 0°C, water exists in its solid state—ice. Although the water molecules in ice crystals stay in fixed positions, they do vibrate. As the molecules are heated, they vibrate faster and the temperature rises.

B Melting
When more energy is added to ice at 0°C, the molecules overcome the forces that keep them in ice crystals. The ice melts or turns to liquid water. As ice melts, the molecules rearrange but do not move faster. Thus, the temperature of the ice stays at 0°C.

C Liquid
Water must be liquid before its temperature can rise above 0°C. As liquid water is heated, the molecules move faster and the temperature rises again.

D Vaporization
When more energy is added to liquid water at 100°C, molecules escape the liquid state and become a gas. This process is called boiling. When water boils, the molecules overcome the forces that hold them together as liquids, but they do not move faster. Thus, the temperature stays at 100°C.

E Gas
Water must be in its gas state—called water vapor—before its temperature can rise above 100°C. As water vapor is heated, the molecules move faster and the temperature rises again.

Figure 28 The matter that makes up the fully grown sunflower plant (right) is the result of a series of chemical reactions that begin when its seed sprouts (below).

Chemical Changes

Changes in state are examples of physical changes. To find an example of chemical changes, you can look at something as simple as a sunflower seed sprouting and growing into the large sunflower in Figure 28.

A sunflower seed is about the size of your fingernail. If conditions are right, however, it will grow into a plant that is taller than you. In time, the sunflower blossom will produce seeds of its own.

Chemical Reactions As a plant grows, it goes through a series of complex chemical reactions. The term **chemical reaction** is another name for a chemical change.

In some chemical reactions, one substance breaks down into two or more other substances. In other reactions, two or more substances combine, forming one or more new substances. The one thing all chemical reactions have in common is that new substances are produced. After a physical change, the substance is the same as the substance you started with.

Energy and Chemical Reactions Like all changes in matter, chemical reactions occur when substances gain or lose energy. All chemical reactions either absorb energy or release energy.

The reactions in plant growth are examples of reactions that absorb energy. Do you know the source of the energy for a plant to grow? The answer is the sun. Plants have substances in them that give the plants the ability to capture light energy. This energy is used to make new plant structures such as leaves, stems, and roots. The plant changes the sun's light energy into the chemical energy of its compounds.

Energy that has been absorbed and stored can be later released. What is an example of a chemical reaction that releases energy? Any burning reaction, such as burning wood in a wood stove or a lit candle, releases energy. Wood, wax, or other fuels combine with oxygen in the air, producing substances such as carbon dioxide, water, soot, and other substances. Light energy and heat are released during this process. Your body releases energy from the foods you eat much more gently then a fire releases energy.

Controlling Chemical Reactions What do you do if you want to make a chemical reaction happen faster or slower? What do you do if you want the reaction to start at a certain time or to stop when you decide? You don't have to be a scientist to control chemical reactions. Sometimes you just have to add energy or take it away.

Think about baking a cake. As soon as you mix the eggs and flour in the bowl, reactions to form new substances start. If the kitchen is warm, reactions in the cake batter happen faster. When you put the cake batter into a hot oven, other reactions begin as heat is transferred to the cake pan. The hotter the oven, the faster the cake bakes. You continue to control chemical reactions by removing the cake from the oven at just the right time. Putting the hot cake on the counter at room temperature allows it to cool. Putting the cake into the refrigerator keeps it fresher and slows down the rate at which it will spoil.

Figure 29 When you mix cake batter and bake a cake, you are controlling reactions.
Interpreting Photos How do these cooks determine when reactions stop or start?

Section 4 Review

1. Compare and contrast physical and chemical changes.
2. How are changes in matter related to changes in energy?
3. Describe how a solid changes into a liquid and how a liquid changes into a gas.
4. Describe the ways that energy can change in a chemical reaction.
5. **Thinking Critically Applying Concepts** If you are stranded in a blizzard and are trying to stay warm, why should you melt snow and then drink it instead of just eating snow?

Check Your Progress

CHAPTER PROJECT 2

Use the information you learned in this section to revise your storyboard, if necessary. Then if you are creating a cartoon, draw the cartoon and write the captions. If you are presenting a skit, write a script and stage directions. Rehearse the skit with the members of your group.

MELTING ICE

In this experiment, you will measure temperature as you explore the melting of ice.

Problem

How does the temperature of the surroundings affect the rate at which ice melts?

Materials

thermometer   stopwatch or timer
2 plastic cups, about 200 mL each
2 stirring rods, preferably plastic
ice cubes, about 2 cm on each side
warm water, about 40°C–45°C

Procedure

1. Read Steps 1–8. Based on your own experience, predict which ice cube will melt faster.
2. In your notebook, make a data table like the one below.
3. Fill a cup halfway with warm water (about 40°C to 45°C). Fill a second cup to the same depth with water at room temperature.
4. Record the exact temperature of the water in each cup.
5. Obtain two ice cubes that are as close to the same size as possible.
6. Place one piece of ice in each cup. Begin timing with a stopwatch. Gently stir each cup with a stirring rod until the ice cube in the cup has completely melted.
7. Observe both ice cubes carefully. At the moment one of the ice cubes is completely melted, record the time and the temperature of the water in the cup.

8. Wait for the second ice cube to melt. Record its melting time and the water temperature.

Analyze and Conclude

1. Was your prediction in Step 1 supported by the results of the experiment? Explain why or why not.
2. In which cup did the water temperature change the most? Explain this result.
3. When the ice melted, its molecules gained enough energy to overcome the forces holding them together as solid ice. What is the source of that energy?
4. **Think About It** How well could you time the exact moment that each ice cube completely melted? How might errors in measurements affect your conclusions?

Design an Experiment

When a lake freezes in winter, only the top layer turns to ice. Design an experiment to model the melting of a frozen lake during the spring. With your teacher's approval, carry out your experiment. Be prepared to share your results with the class.

DATA TABLE

	Beginning Temperature (°C)	Time to Melt (s)	Final Temperature (°C)
Cup 1			
Cup 2			

SECTION 1 Solids, Liquids, and Gases

Key Ideas

- Solids have a definite shape and volume because the particles in a solid are packed tightly together and stay in fixed positions.
- The particles in a liquid are free to move around one another. Thus, a liquid has no definite shape, but it does have a definite volume.
- The particles of a gas spread apart to fill all the space available to them. Thus, a gas has neither definite shape nor definite volume.

Key Terms

solid	fluid
crystalline solid	viscosity
amorphous solid	gas
liquid	

SECTION 2 Behavior of Gases

Key Ideas

- Volume, temperature, and pressure are three different properties of a gas you can measure.
- When the volume of a gas decreases, its pressure increases. This relationship is explained by Boyle's law.
- In a rigid container, raising the temperature of a gas increases its pressure.
- In a flexible container, raising the temperature of a gas increases its volume. This relationship is explained by Charles's law.

Key Terms

temperature	Boyle's law
pressure	Charles's law

SECTION 3 Graphing Gas Behavior

INTEGRATING MATHEMATICS

Key Ideas

- When values for the volume and kelvin temperature of a gas under constant pressure are graphed, the graph shows that the volume and temperature are directly proportional.
- When values for the volume and pressure of a gas are graphed, the points fall in a downward curve. The graph shows that the pressure of a gas varies inversely with its volume.

Key Terms

graph	vary inversely
directly proportional	

SECTION 4 Physical and Chemical Changes

Key Ideas

- In a physical change, substances change form but not their identities. In a chemical change, substances change into other substances.
- Matter changes whenever energy is added to or taken away from it.
- Changes of state occur when a substance gains or loses energy and the particles of the substance are rearranged.
- Chemical changes are also called chemical reactions. Chemical reactions either absorb or release energy.

Key Terms

thermal energy	vaporization
chemical energy	evaporation
law of conservation	boiling
of energy	condensation
melting	sublimation
freezing	chemical reaction

USING THE INTERNET

ACTIVITY

www.science-explorer.phschool.com

Reviewing Content

For more review of key concepts, see the Interactive Student Tutorial CD-ROM.

Multiple Choice

Choose the letter of the answer that best completes each statement.

1. A substance with a definite volume but no definite shape is a
   a. crystalline solid.
   b. liquid.
   c. gas.
   d. amorphous solid.

2. Unlike solids and liquids, a gas will
   a. keep its volume in different containers.
   b. keep its shape in different containers.
   c. expand to fill the space available to it.
   d. have its volume decrease when the temperature rises.

3. According to Boyle's law, the volume of a gas increases when its
   a. pressure increases.
   b. pressure decreases.
   c. temperature falls.
   d. temperature rises.

4. The vertical axis of a graph shows the
   a. responding variable.
   b. manipulated variable.
   c. constant factors.
   d. same variable as the *x*-axis.

5. Lighting a match is an example of a
   a. physical change.
   b. change of state.
   c. change in gas pressure.
   d. chemical change.

True or False

If the statement is true, write true. If it is false, change the underlined word or words to make it a true statement.

6. Rubber and glass become softer and softer over a wide range of temperatures. They are examples of <u>crystalline</u> solids.

7. The energy from the movement of particles is measured by the <u>temperature</u> of a substance.

8. If a gas is contained in a rigid container, raising its temperature will increase its <u>volume</u>.

9. According to Boyle's law, the volume of a gas varies <u>directly</u> with its pressure.

10. When you see steam, fog, or clouds, you see water in the <u>gas</u> state.

Checking Concepts

11. Describe the motion of particles in a solid.
12. Why can liquids flow from place to place?
13. Compare and contrast liquids with high and low viscosities.
14. How is the temperature of a substance related to the energy of movement of the particles in the substance?
15. What happens to the gas particles when the air in an inflated ball leaks out?
16. List four examples of types of energy.
17. What happens to water molecules when water is heated from 90°C to 110°C?
18. Compare the processes of melting and freezing.
19. **Writing to Learn** Imagine you are Robert Boyle or Jacques Charles at the time you described the law that came to be known by your name. Tell the story of your experiments and results as you think Boyle or Charles would if he could talk to the students in your class today. Write down exactly what you would say.

Thinking Visually

20. **Compare/Contrast Table** Copy the compare/contrast table about the states of matter onto a separate sheet of paper. Then complete it and add a title. (For more on compare/contrast tables, see the Skills Handbook.)

State of Matter	Shape	Volume	Example (at room temperature)
a. _?_	Definite	b. _?_	Diamond
Liquid	c. _?_	Definite	d. _?_
Gas	e. _?_	Not definite	f. _?_

Applying Skills

After each 10°C change in temperature, the mass of lead nitrate dissolved in 100 mL of water was measured. Use this data to answer Questions 21–23.

Temperature (°C)	Lead Nitrate Dissolved (g)
0	37
10	47
20	56
30	66
40	75

21. Graphing Graph the data for mass dissolved at each temperature. Label the horizontal axis from 0°C to 60°C and the vertical axis from 0 grams to 100 grams.

22. Interpreting Data What does the graph show about the effect of temperature on the amount of lead nitrate that will dissolve in water?

23. Predicting Assume the amount of lead nitrate dissolved continues to increase as the water is heated. Predict how many grams dissolve at 50°C.

Thinking Critically

24. Relating Cause and Effect Explain why placing a dented table tennis ball in boiling water is one way to remove a dent in the ball. Assume it has no holes.

25. Comparing and Contrasting Using diagrams, show the gas particles in an air mattress before you lie down on it and while you are lying on it.

26. Applying Concepts The explosion of dynamite is a chemical reaction. Does this reaction absorb or release energy? Explain.

27. Classifying Decide whether each of the following is a physical or chemical change: a log rotting on the forest floor, alcohol expanding in a thermometer on a hot day, a plastic toy bending into different positions, water breaking apart into hydrogen gas and oxygen gas.

28. Making Generalizations When you open a solid room air freshener, the solid slowly loses mass and volume. How do you think this happens?

Performance Assessment

CHAPTER PROJECT 2

Wrap Up

Present Your Project If you prepared a cartoon, read the captions to the class and discuss the illustrations. If you prepared a skit, perform the skit in front of the class. After you finish your presentation, invite the class to ask questions about your project. Be prepared to share the decisions you made in creating your presentation.

Reflect and Record In your journal, describe the strengths and weaknesses of the way you modeled changes of state. How successful was your model? How well did your classmates understand your cartoon or skit? Describe what you learned from observing the projects of your classmates.

Getting Involved

In Your School Make a survey of the sporting equipment in your school. Which pieces of equipment need to be inflated with air? Examine the label on each piece. Is there a pressure recommended for inflation? What happens if an item is underinflated? What happens if it is overinflated? Make a table showing your results.

In some ways the periodic table is like this system for organizing yarn.

WHAT'S AHEAD

PROJECT 3

Getting Organized

Imagine searching for matching skeins of yarn if all the yarn had been tossed randomly into a large bin. Luckily, the owner of the store has grouped the yarn by color and by the thickness of the yarn strands. You may have seen similar systems of organization in other stores or in your own home. Chemists also have a system of organization—a system for organizing the elements. There are more than 100 elements. As you will learn in this chapter, about 80 elements are classified as metals. In this project, you will examine the properties of different metals more closely.

Your Goal To survey the properties of several metal samples.

To complete the project you must
◆ interpret what the periodic table tells you about your samples
◆ design and conduct experiments that will allow you to test at least three properties of your metals
◆ compare and contrast the properties of your sample metals
◆ follow the safety guidelines in Appendix A

Get Started Begin by brainstorming with your classmates about metals. How do you think metals differ from nonmetals? Your teacher will assign samples of metals to your group. You will be observing their properties in this project.

Check Your Progress You'll be working on this project as you study this chapter. To keep your project on track, look for Check Your Progress boxes at the following points.
Section 1 Review, page 86: Extract information from the periodic table.
Section 2 Review, page 92: Design experiments to test for properties.
Section 4 Review, page 106: Conduct tests on all samples.

Wrap Up At the end of the chapter (page 109), you will prepare a presentation comparing and contrasting the expected and observed properties of the metals you investigated.

SECTION 4

Integrating Space Science
Elements From Stardust

Discover **Can Helium Be Made From Hydrogen?**

DISCOVER

ACTIVITY

Which Is Easier?

1. Make 4 sets of 10 paper squares, using a different color for each set. Number the squares in each set from 1 through 10.

2. Place all of the squares on a flat surface, numbered side up. Don't arrange them in order.

3. Ask your partner to name a square by color and number. Have your partner time how long it takes you to find this square.

4. Repeat Step 3 twice, choosing different squares each time. Calculate the average value of the three times.

5. Rearrange the squares into four rows, one for each color. Order the squares in each row from 1 to 10.

6. Repeat Step 3 three times. Calculate an average time.

7. Trade places with your partner and repeat Steps 2 through 6.

Think It Over

Inferring Which average time was shorter, the one produced in Step 4 or Step 6? Why do you think the times were different?

GUIDE FOR READING

◆ How was the periodic table developed?

◆ What information does the periodic table present?

◆ How are valence electrons related to the periodic table?

Reading Tip As you read this section, refer to *Exploring the Periodic Table* on pages 80–81. Look for patterns.

You wake up, jump out of bed, and start to get dressed for school. Then you ask yourself a question: Is there school today? To find out, you check the calendar. There's no school today because it's Saturday.

The calendar arranges the days of the month into horizontal periods called weeks and vertical groups called days of the week. Just as Monday always starts the school week, Saturday always starts the weekend. The calendar is useful because it organizes the days of the year. In the same way that days can be organized into a calendar, the elements can be organized into something like a calendar. As you'll discover in this section, the name of the "chemists' calendar" is the periodic table.

Looking for Patterns in the Elements

As you have learned, matter is made of about 100 different elements that have a wide variety of properties. Some elements are very reactive—they form compounds readily with other elements. Other elements are less reactive. And still other elements do not form compounds at all.

Mendeleev, the Detective

In the 1800s, scientists began to suspect that the elements could be organized in a useful way. By 1869, one Russian scientist recognized a hidden pattern in the elements. His name was Dmitri Mendeleev (men duh LAY ef). Like any good detective, Mendeleev studied the evidence, considered each clue, and looked for patterns.

One of his first observations was that some elements have similar chemical and physical properties. Fluorine and chlorine, for example, are both gases that irritate your lungs if you breathe them. Silver and copper are both shiny metals that gradually tarnish if exposed to air. Mendeleev believed that these similarities were important clues to the pattern he was looking for. To help him find the pattern, Mendeleev wrote facts about the elements on individual paper cards. He wrote all the properties he knew about an element, including its melting point, density, and color.

Mendeleev also recorded two other important properties: atomic mass and bonding power. The **atomic mass** of an element is the average mass of one atom of the element. In Mendeleev's day, scientists figured out atomic masses in comparison to hydrogen, the lightest element. Bonding power refers to the number of chemical bonds an element can form. This was determined by studying how each element formed compounds with oxygen.

Figure 1 The shiny orange of this copper bowl will gradually turn to dull blue-green, like the tarnished copper sculpture. Mendeleev realized that several metals share with copper the property of tarnishing when exposed to air.
Classifying Is tarnishing a physical or chemical property?

The First Periodic Table

Mendeleev liked to play Patience, a solitaire card game, so he had practice in seeing patterns. He tried arranging his cards on the elements in various ways. **Mendeleev noticed that patterns appeared when the elements were arranged in order of increasing atomic mass.** He also discovered that the bonding power of the elements from lithium to fluorine change in an orderly way.

Figure 2 Mendeleev arranged the elements in order of atomic mass. The positive and negative numbers stand for the elements' bonding powers.

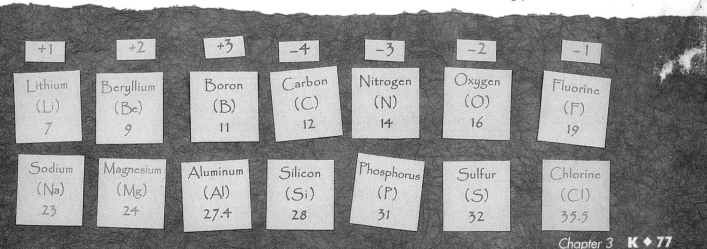

+1	+2	+3	−4	−3	−2	−1
Lithium (Li) 7	Beryllium (Be) 9	Boron (B) 11	Carbon (C) 12	Nitrogen (N) 14	Oxygen (O) 16	Fluorine (F) 19
Sodium (Na) 23	Magnesium (Mg) 24	Aluminum (Al) 27.4	Silicon (Si) 28	Phosphorus (P) 31	Sulfur (S) 32	Chlorine (Cl) 35.5

Figure 3 Mendeleev (far right) published this first periodic table in 1869. He left question marks in some places. Based on the properties and atomic masses of surrounding elements, he predicted that new elements with specific characteristics would be discovered. *Comparing and Contrasting How is Mendeleev's chart similar to and different from the modern periodic table in Exploring the Periodic Table?*

				Ti=50	Zr=90	?=180.
				V=51	Nb=94	Ta=182.
				Cr=52	Mo=96	W=186.
				Mn=55	Rh=104,4	Pt=197,4
				Fe=56	Ru=104,4	Ir=198.
			Ni=Co=59		Pl=106₆,	Os=199.
H=1				Cu=63,4	Ag=108	Hg=200.
	Be=9,4	Mg=24	Zn=65,2	Cd=112		
	B=11	Al=27,4	?=68	Ur=116	Au=197?	
	C=12	Si=28	?=70	Sn=118		
	N=14	P=31	As=75	Sb=122	Bi=210	
	O=16	S=32	Se=79,4	Te=128?		
	F=19	Cl=35,5	Br=80	I=127		
Li=7	Na=23	K=39	Rb=85,4	Cs=133	Tl=204	
		Ca=40	Sr=57,6	Ba=137	Pb=207	
		?=45	Ce=92			
		?Er=56	La=94			
		?Yt=60	Di=95			
		?In=75,6	Th=118?			

After fluorine, the next heaviest element Mendeleev knew was sodium. (Neon had yet to be discovered.) The bonding power of sodium is the same as that of lithium. Mendeleev grouped the card for sodium with the card for lithium. As he laid out cards, each element had properties similar to those of the other elements in its group.

As Mendeleev discovered, arranging the elements by increasing atomic mass does not produce a perfect table. So he moved cards to positions where they fit best. However, this left three blank spaces. Mendeleev boldly proposed that the blank spaces would be filled by elements that had not yet been discovered! He even predicted their properties.

In 1869, Mendeleev published the first periodic table of the elements, shown in Figure 3. The word *periodic* means "a regular, repeated pattern." In the modern **periodic table,** the properties of the elements repeat in each row—or period—of the table. Within 16 years, chemists had discovered all three of the missing elements, which were named scandium, gallium, and germanium. Their properties are very close to what Mendeleev had predicted.

☑ *Checkpoint* *What does "periodic" mean?*

The Periodic Table and the Atom

In the years after Mendeleev, chemists made many discoveries that required changes in the periodic table. The most important of these changes came in the early 1900s, when scientists began to identify the particles that make up atoms.

Classifying ACTIVITY
Choose any 10 elements and assign them letters *A* through *J*. On an index card for each element, write the letter for the element and list some of its properties. You may list properties that you learned in this chapter, or list properties presented in an encyclopedia or other reference source.

Exchange cards with a classmate. Can you identify each element? Which properties are the most helpful in identifying elements?

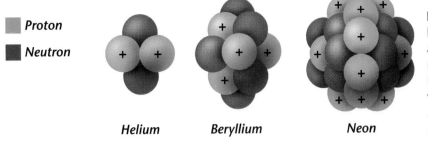

Proton
Neutron

Helium   Beryllium   Neon

Figure 4 The nuclei of helium, beryllium, and neon all contain protons and neutrons. Yet helium, beryllium, and neon are very different elements. *Applying Concepts What accounts for these differences?*

Inside an Atom Deep within every atom is a core called a **nucleus** (plural *nuclei*). The model of the atom used today shows the nucleus as containing smaller particles called **protons** and **neutrons.** Outside the nucleus are other particles, called **electrons.**

Because atoms are so small, they cannot be measured with everyday units of mass. For this reason, scientists have created the **atomic mass unit** (amu) to measure the particles in atoms. The mass of a proton or a neutron is about one atomic mass unit. A proton has almost two thousand times the mass of an electron, which means that most of an atom's mass is in its nucleus. Thus, an atom that contains 3 protons, 4 neutrons, and 3 electrons has a mass of about 7 atomic mass units.

Protons and electrons also carry electrical charges. Neutrons, as their name implies, are neutral—they carry no charge. Protons carry a positive electrical charge. Electrons carry a negative electrical charge. In addition, electrons move constantly and rapidly in the space around the nucleus. The fact that electrons move is very important—how important will become clear as you read on.

Atomic Number Every atom of a particular element contains the same number of protons. For example, every carbon atom contains six protons. Thus, an element's **atomic number**—the number of protons in its nucleus—is a unique property that identifies that element.

However, the atoms of an element may vary in the number of neutrons they contain. A carbon atom, for instance, may have five, six, seven, or eight neutrons. That means that the mass of atoms of an element can vary. For these reasons, and because differences in mass could not explain the way specific elements react, chemists now organize the periodic table according to atomic number instead of atomic mass.

The Periodic Table Today Although the periodic table is now arranged according to atomic number, the modern version of the table is like Mendeleev's table in many ways. However, it now contains more than 100 elements. Take some time to examine some of those elements and how they are arranged in *Exploring the Periodic Table* on the next two pages.

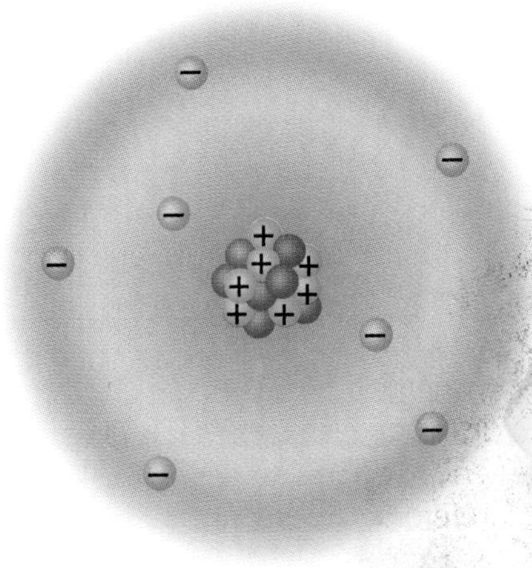

Figure 5 This nitrogen atom is composed of 7 protons, 7 neutrons, and 7 electrons. The electrons move in the space around the nucleus in a fuzzy, cloudlike blur.

EXPLORING the Periodic Table

The periodic table has grown to include over 100 elements. Once you understand how the periodic table is organized, you can predict an element's properties from its position in the table.

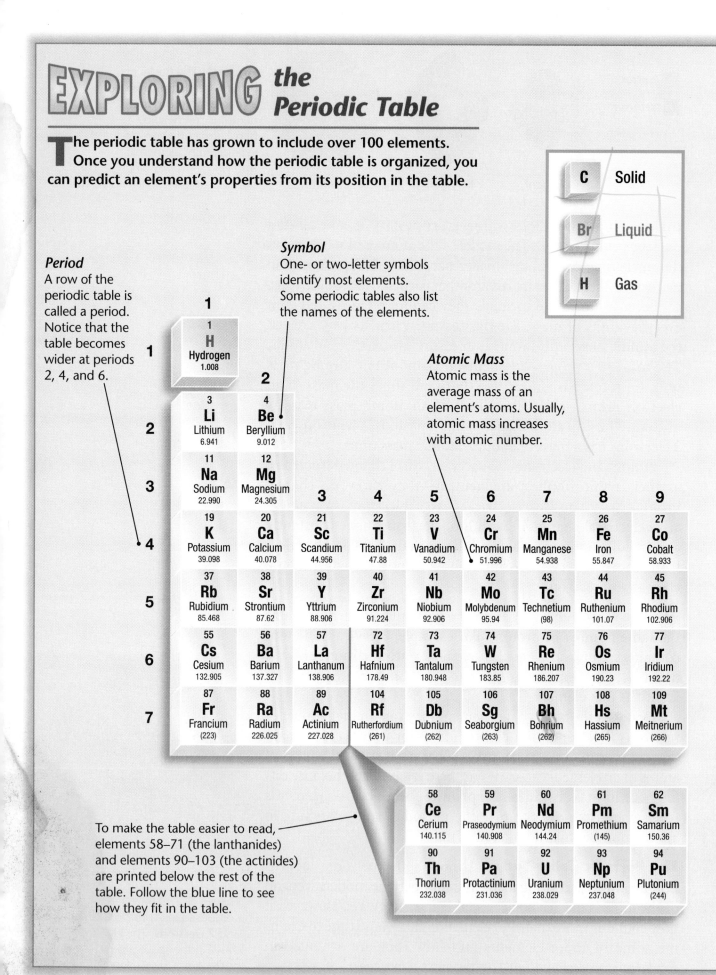

Period
A row of the periodic table is called a period. Notice that the table becomes wider at periods 2, 4, and 6.

Symbol
One- or two-letter symbols identify most elements. Some periodic tables also list the names of the elements.

Atomic Mass
Atomic mass is the average mass of an element's atoms. Usually, atomic mass increases with atomic number.

C	Solid
Br	Liquid
H	Gas

1
1
H
Hydrogen
1.008

2
3	4
Li	**Be**
Lithium	Beryllium
6.941	9.012
11	12
Na	**Mg**
Sodium	Magnesium
22.990	24.305

3	4	5	6	7	8	9
21	22	23	24	25	26	27
Sc	**Ti**	**V**	**Cr**	**Mn**	**Fe**	**Co**
Scandium	Titanium	Vanadium	Chromium	Manganese	Iron	Cobalt
44.956	47.88	50.942	51.996	54.938	55.847	58.933
39	40	41	42	43	44	45
Y	**Zr**	**Nb**	**Mo**	**Tc**	**Ru**	**Rh**
Yttrium	Zirconium	Niobium	Molybdenum	Technetium	Ruthenium	Rhodium
88.906	91.224	92.906	95.94	(98)	101.07	102.906
57	72	73	74	75	76	77
La	**Hf**	**Ta**	**W**	**Re**	**Os**	**Ir**
Lanthanum	Hafnium	Tantalum	Tungsten	Rhenium	Osmium	Iridium
138.906	178.49	180.948	183.85	186.207	190.23	192.22
89	104	105	106	107	108	109
Ac	**Rf**	**Db**	**Sg**	**Bh**	**Hs**	**Mt**
Actinium	Rutherfordium	Dubnium	Seaborgium	Bohrium	Hassium	Meitnerium
227.028	(261)	(262)	(263)	(262)	(265)	(266)

Period column (row labels): 1, 2, 3, 4, 5, 6, 7

Row 4 (period 4): 19 **K** Potassium 39.098 | 20 **Ca** Calcium 40.078
Row 5 (period 5): 37 **Rb** Rubidium 85.468 | 38 **Sr** Strontium 87.62
Row 6 (period 6): 55 **Cs** Cesium 132.905 | 56 **Ba** Barium 137.327
Row 7 (period 7): 87 **Fr** Francium (223) | 88 **Ra** Radium 226.025

58	59	60	61	62
Ce	**Pr**	**Nd**	**Pm**	**Sm**
Cerium	Praseodymium	Neodymium	Promethium	Samarium
140.115	140.908	144.24	(145)	150.36
90	91	92	93	94
Th	**Pa**	**U**	**Np**	**Pu**
Thorium	Protactinium	Uranium	Neptunium	Plutonium
232.038	231.036	238.029	237.048	(244)

To make the table easier to read, elements 58–71 (the lanthanides) and elements 90–103 (the actinides) are printed below the rest of the table. Follow the blue line to see how they fit in the table.

Chemical Symbol Parade
(con't)

13. Boron   Chromium   Iodine

_____   _____   _____

14. Hydrogen   Argon   Nitrogen

_____   _____   _____

Aluminum   Tungsten

_____   _____

15. Sulfur   Phosphorus   Nitrogen

_____   _____   _____

Oxygen   Erbium

_____   _____

16. Iridium   Phosphorus   Tantalum

_____   _____   _____

17. Ruthenium   Sulfur   Tungsten

_____   _____   _____

Aluminum

_____

18. Calcium   Indium   Boron

_____   _____   _____

19. Sodium   Titanium   Rhenium

_____   _____   _____

20. Titanium   Carbon   Actinium

_____   _____   _____

13. A baby's bed. _____

14. A large sea animal related to the dolphin. _____

15. An individual. _____

16. A nocturnal hoofed mammal with a long flexible snout.

_____

17. Large northern sea mammal.

_____

18. A private room on a ship.

_____

19. Sensory membrane of the eye.

_____

20. More than one flowering plant of the desert.

_____

Name _____ Date _____

79. Chemical Symbol Parade

Find the chemical symbols for the elements listed in each group below. Write the symbol in the space under each element. Then put the symbols together to spell the name of the mystery word. Use the clues and a periodic table to help you.

1. Arsenic   Phosphorus   Chlorine

_____   _____   _____

2. Thorium   Protactinium

_____   _____

3. Cerium   Radium

_____   _____

4. Nitrogen   Cobalt   Radium   Oxygen

_____   _____   _____   _____

5. Dysprosium   Boron   Oxygen

_____   _____   _____

   Nitrogen   Oxygen

   _____   _____

6. Lanthanum   Cerium   Nitrogen

_____   _____   _____

7. Oxygen   Carbon   Boron   Radium

_____   _____   _____   _____

8. Barium   Rhodium   Rubidium   Uranium

_____   _____   _____   _____

9. Erbium   Oxygen   Rhodium

_____   _____   _____

   Osmium   Carbon   Indium

   _____   _____   _____

10. Argon   Nitrogen   Lutetium

_____   _____   _____

11. Nitrogen   Bromine   Oxygen   Cobalt

_____   _____   _____   _____

12. Erbium   Polonium   Potassium

_____   _____   _____

1. A hook for holding objects together. _____

2. A route or course.

_____

3. Horses in a contest.

_____

4. Small, gray animal with a bushy ringed tail. _____

5. Not anybody. _____

6. A knight's weapon.

_____

7. A hooded poisonous snake.

_____

8. Broad green-leaf plants with thick, juicy, pink stems. _____

9. Large plant-eating African mammal. _____

10. Relating to the moon.

_____

11. A partly broken range horse.

_____

12. A card game. _____

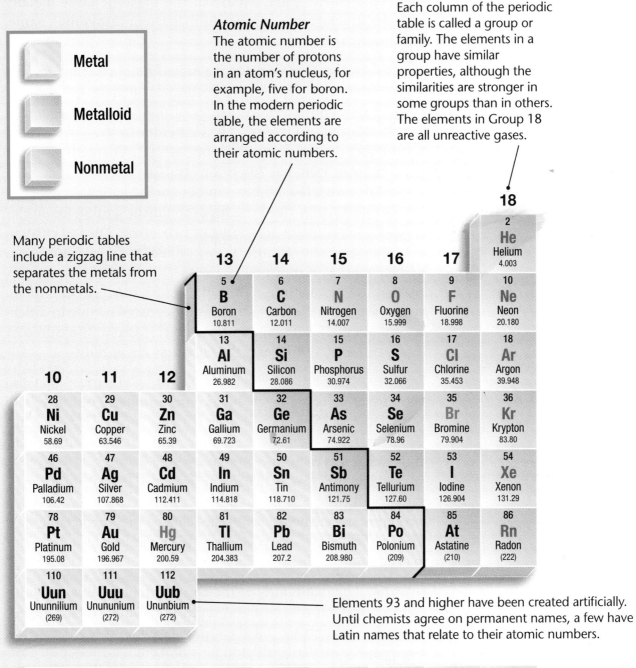

Metal

Metalloid

Nonmetal

Atomic Number
The atomic number is the number of protons in an atom's nucleus, for example, five for boron. In the modern periodic table, the elements are arranged according to their atomic numbers.

Family
Each column of the periodic table is called a group or family. The elements in a group have similar properties, although the similarities are stronger in some groups than in others. The elements in Group 18 are all unreactive gases.

Many periodic tables include a zigzag line that separates the metals from the nonmetals.

Elements 93 and higher have been created artificially. Until chemists agree on permanent names, a few have Latin names that relate to their atomic numbers.

13	14	15	16	17	18
					2 **He** Helium 4.003
5 **B** Boron 10.811	6 **C** Carbon 12.011	7 **N** Nitrogen 14.007	8 **O** Oxygen 15.999	9 **F** Fluorine 18.998	10 **Ne** Neon 20.180
13 **Al** Aluminum 26.982	14 **Si** Silicon 28.086	15 **P** Phosphorus 30.974	16 **S** Sulfur 32.066	17 **Cl** Chlorine 35.453	18 **Ar** Argon 39.948

10	11	12						
28 **Ni** Nickel 58.69	29 **Cu** Copper 63.546	30 **Zn** Zinc 65.39	31 **Ga** Gallium 69.723	32 **Ge** Germanium 72.61	33 **As** Arsenic 74.922	34 **Se** Selenium 78.96	35 **Br** Bromine 79.904	36 **Kr** Krypton 83.80
46 **Pd** Palladium 106.42	47 **Ag** Silver 107.868	48 **Cd** Cadmium 112.411	49 **In** Indium 114.818	50 **Sn** Tin 118.710	51 **Sb** Antimony 121.75	52 **Te** Tellurium 127.60	53 **I** Iodine 126.904	54 **Xe** Xenon 131.29
78 **Pt** Platinum 195.08	79 **Au** Gold 196.967	80 **Hg** Mercury 200.59	81 **Tl** Thallium 204.383	82 **Pb** Lead 207.2	83 **Bi** Bismuth 208.980	84 **Po** Polonium (209)	85 **At** Astatine (210)	86 **Rn** Radon (222)
110 **Uun** Ununnilium (269)	111 **Uuu** Unununium (272)	112 **Uub** Ununbium (272)						

63 **Eu** Europium 151.965	64 **Gd** Gadolinium 157.25	65 **Tb** Terbium 158.925	66 **Dy** Dysprosium 162.50	67 **Ho** Holmium 164.930	68 **Er** Erbium 167.26	69 **Tm** Thulium 168.934	70 **Yb** Ytterbium 173.04	71 **Lu** Lutetium 174.967
95 **Am** Americium (243)	96 **Cm** Curium (247)	97 **Bk** Berkelium (247)	98 **Cf** Californium (251)	99 **Es** Einsteinium (252)	100 **Fm** Fermium (257)	101 **Md** Mendelevium (258)	102 **No** Nobelium (259)	103 **Lr** Lawrencium (260)

Reading the Periodic Table

The periodic table contains over 100 squares, one separate square for each element. **Each square of the periodic table usually includes the element's atomic number, chemical symbol, name, and atomic mass.**

Figure 6 Four important facts about an element are supplied in each square of the periodic table.

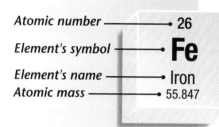

Atomic number ———————→ 26
Element's symbol ———————→ **Fe**
Element's name ———————→ Iron
Atomic mass ———————→ 55.847

Inside the Squares On the periodic table on the previous two pages, find the square for iron, located in the top position in column 8 in the center of the table. That square is reproduced in Figure 6. The first entry in the square is the number 26, the atomic number of iron. That tells you that every iron atom has 26 protons and 26 electrons.

Just below the atomic number are the letters Fe, which is the chemical symbol for iron. Every **chemical symbol** for an element usually contains either one or two letters. The last entry in the square is the atomic mass, which is 55.847 for iron. Remember that atomic mass is the average mass of an element's atoms. Some iron atoms have a mass of 55, others a mass of 56, and still others a mass of 57. These differences are due to different numbers of neutrons in the nuclei. Despite the different masses, all iron atoms react the same way chemically.

Organization of the Periodic Table Remember that the periodic table is arranged by atomic number. Look over the entire table, starting at the top left with hydrogen (H), which has atomic number 1. Follow the atomic numbers from left to right, and read across each row.

An element's properties can be predicted from its location in the periodic table. As you look at elements across a row or down a column, the elements' properties change in a predictable way. This predictability is the reason why the periodic table is so useful to chemists.

Groups The main body of the periodic table is arranged into eighteen vertical columns and seven horizontal rows. The elements in a column are called a **group.** Groups are also known as **families.** Notice that each group is numbered, from Group 1 on the left of the table to Group 18 on the right. Typically, the group is given a family name based on the first element in the column. Group 14, for example, is the carbon family. Group 15 is the nitrogen family.

The elements in each group, or family, have similar characteristics. The elements in Group 1 are all metals that react violently with water. The metals in Group 11 all react with water slowly or not at all. Group 17 elements react violently with elements from Group 1, while Group 18 elements rarely react at all.

Language Arts
CONNECTION

You are learning science in the English language. But in other centuries, the language of science was Greek or Latin or even Arabic. This is why the names and chemical symbols of many elements don't match modern names. For example, the symbol for iron (Fe) comes from the Latin *ferrum.*

In Your Journal

List some of the elements that have puzzling chemical symbols, such as sodium (Na), potassium (K), tin (Sn), gold (Au), silver (Ag), lead (Pb), and mercury (Hg). Look up these names and symbols in the dictionary to learn the original names of these elements.

Periods Each horizontal row across the table is called a **period.** A period contains a series of different types of elements from different families, just as a week on a calendar has a series of different days. Unlike the elements in a family, the elements in each period are not alike in properties. In fact, as you move across a period, the elements gradually change properties. But there is a pattern as you move across a period from left to right.

In the fourth period, for example, the elements change from very reactive metals, such as potassium (K) and calcium (Ca), to relatively unreactive metals, such as nickel (Ni) and copper (Cu), to metalloids and nonmetals, such as arsenic (As) and bromine (Br). The last element in a period is always a particularly inactive gas. In this period, that element is krypton (Kr). Krypton bears no relationship to the fictional substance Kryptonite, which is the only thing feared by Superman!

As you can see, there are seven periods of elements. Periods have different numbers of elements. Period 1 has only two elements, hydrogen (H) and helium (He). You can count that Periods 2 and 3 each have 8 elements. Periods 4 and 5 each have 18 elements.

You will also notice that some elements of Period 6 and some elements of Period 7 have been separated out of the table. These elements are part of the periodic table, even though they appear as rows below its main section. The elements are shown separately to keep the table from becoming too wide. Imagine what it would look like if Periods 6 and 7 were stretched out to show all 32 elements in a row.

Figure 7 You can find the names of elements in the names of some common products, such as the ni-cad batteries in this camera. *Inferring What is one of the metals you would expect to find in a ni-cad battery?*

☑ *Checkpoint* *What is the name for a column of elements in the periodic table?*

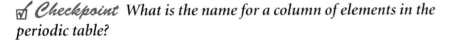
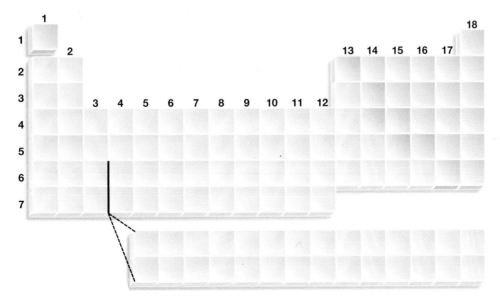

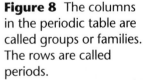

Figure 8 The columns in the periodic table are called groups or families. The rows are called periods.

Why the Table Works

You saw that Mendeleev used the property of bonding power when developing his periodic table. Bonding power refers to the number of bonds an element forms during a chemical change. But Mendeleev could not explain bonding power because he did not know about the structure of atoms.

Valence Electrons   Recall that in an atom, protons and neutrons make up the nucleus, while electrons are outside the nucleus. It is the electrons that explain bonding power because electrons can be shared between or transferred to other atoms. But this is

Discovery of the Elements

In 1869, when Dmitri Mendeleev developed his first periodic table, 63 elements were known. Since then, scientists have discovered or created nearly 50 new elements.

1875
Gallium

Mendeleev had predicted the properties of an unknown element that he called "eka-aluminum," which would fit directly below aluminum in the table. In 1875, French chemist Paul-Émile Lecoq de Boisbaudran discovered an element, which he called gallium, with the properties that Mendeleev had predicted.

1898
Polonium and Radium

Polish chemist Marie Curie started with three tons of uranium ore before she eventually isolated a few grams of two new elements, which she named polonium and radium.

1850   **1880**   **1910**

1894
Argon, Neon, Krypton, and Xenon

British chemist Sir William Ramsay discovered an element he named argon, after the Greek word for lazy. The name is appropriate because argon does not react with other elements. Ramsay started looking for other nonreactive gases and eventually discovered neon, krypton, and xenon.

not true for all electrons. When an atom has two or more electrons, the electrons may be at different distances from the nucleus. Only the electrons that are farthest out can be shared or transferred. Electrons that are involved in transfer or sharing are called **valence electrons.**

Elements may have different numbers of valence electrons. The number of valence electrons determines whether the element gives up, shares, or accepts electrons. The number of valence electrons an element has increases from left to right across a period.

In Your Journal

Select three elements that interest you and find out more about them. Who identified or discovered the elements? How did the elements get their names? How are the elements used? To answer these questions, look up the elements in a reference book.

1941
Plutonium

American chemist Glenn Seaborg was the first to isolate plutonium, which is found in small amounts in uranium ores. Plutonium is used as fuel in certain types of nuclear reactors. It has also been used to provide energy for small power units in space exploration.

1940　　　**1970**　　　**2000**

1939
Francium

Although Mendeleev predicted the properties of an element he called "eka-cesium," the element was not discovered until 1939. French chemist Marguerite Perey named her discovery after the country France.

1997
Elements 101 to 109

The International Union of Pure and Applied Chemists (IUPAC) agreed on official names for elements 101 to 109. Many of the names honor important scientists, such as Lise Meitner, shown here in 1913. All of the new elements were created artificially in laboratories, and none is stable enough to exist in nature.

Group 1

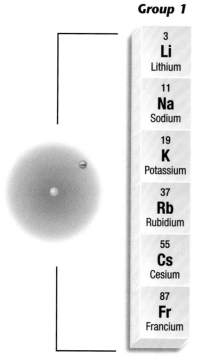

3
Li
Lithium

11
Na
Sodium

19
K
Potassium

37
Rb
Rubidium

55
Cs
Cesium

87
Fr
Francium

Group 17

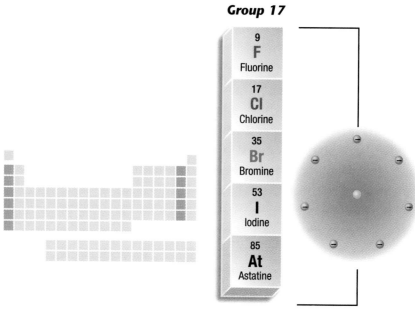

9
F
Fluorine

17
Cl
Chlorine

35
Br
Bromine

53
I
Iodine

85
At
Astatine

Figure 9 All the elements in one group have the same number of valence electrons.
Making Generalizations What do the elements in Group 1 have in common? What do the elements in Group 17 have in common?

Valence Electrons in Groups Atoms that have the same number and arrangement of valence electrons have similar properties, which is why the elements fall into a periodic pattern. **The elements in each group of the periodic table have the same number and arrangement of valence electrons.**

For example, each of the elements in Group 1, at the far left of the table, has atoms with 1 valence electron. In Group 18, at the far right side of the table, each element except helium has atoms with 8 valence electrons.

In Sections 2 and 3, you will explore each group of elements and learn about their properties. As you read about a group of elements, think about how many valence electrons there are in the atoms.

Section 1 Review

1. How did Mendeleev organize the elements into the periodic table? by ~~mass~~ atomic #
2. What information is listed in each square of the periodic table? atomic #, name chemical
3. What does the periodic table tell you about the ~~gas~~ symbol elements in a group?
4. **Thinking Critically Comparing and Contrasting** Element A is in the same group as element B and the same period as element C. Which two of the three elements are likely to have similar properties? Explain your answer. the ones next to each other

Check Your Progress
Find the squares in the periodic table for each metal that you have been assigned. Prepare a chart in which to record the chemical symbol, group number, atomic number, and atomic mass of the metals, as well as their characteristic properties. Record data from the periodic table in your chart.

CHAPTER PROJECT
3

SECTION 2 Metals

Why Use Aluminum?

1. Examine several objects made from aluminum including a can, a disposable pie plate, heavy-duty aluminum foil, foil wrapping paper, and aluminum wire.

2. Compare the shape, thickness, and general appearance of the objects.

3. Observe what happens if you try to bend and unbend each object.

4. For what purpose is each object used?

Think It Over

Inferring Use your observations to list as many properties of aluminum as you can. Based on your list of properties, infer why aluminum was used to make each object. Which objects do you think could be made from other metals? Explain your answer.

Metals are all around you. The cars and buses you ride in are made of steel, which is mostly iron. Airplanes are made of aluminum. Many coins are combinations of zinc with copper, nickel, or silver. Copper wires carry electricity into table lamps, stereos, and computers. It's hard to imagine life without metals.

What Is a Metal?

Look at the periodic table, either in Section 1 or in Appendix D. Most of the elements are metals, found to the left of the zigzag line in the periodic table. The other elements are classified as nonmetals and metalloids. You'll learn more about non-metals and metalloids in the next section.

Physical Properties What is a metal? Take a moment to describe a familiar metal, such as iron, tin, gold, or silver. What words did you use—hard, shiny, smooth? **Chemists classify an element as a metal based on physical properties such as hardness, shininess, malleability, and ductility.** Polished silver (Ag) is a good example of shininess. A **malleable** material is one that can be pounded into shapes. A **ductile** material is one that can be pulled out, or drawn, into a long wire. Copper sheeting and copper wires can be made because of copper's malleability and ductility.

GUIDE FOR READING

◆ What are the properties of metals?

◆ How can you characterize each family of metals?

Reading Tip As you read the name of a new metal or group of metals, find its location on the periodic table.

Robot handling metal heart valves ▶

Figure 10 Because it is shiny and slow to react, chromium is ideal for car bumpers. Other metals are magnetic, like the iron in these paper clips.

Most metals are called good **conductors** because they transmit heat and electricity easily. Several metals are attracted to magnets and can be made into magnets. Thus, iron (Fe), cobalt (Co), and nickel (Ni) are described as **magnetic.**

Most metals are solids at room temperatures. This is because most metals have the property of very high melting points. In fact, you would need to raise the temperature of some metals as high as 3,400°C to melt them. An exception is mercury (Hg), which is a liquid at room temperature.

Chemical Properties **Metals show a wide range of chemical properties.** The ease and speed with which an element combines, or reacts, with other elements and compounds is called its **reactivity.** Some metals are very reactive. For example, sodium (Na) and potassium (K) must be stored under oil in sealed containers. If exposed to air or water, they can react explosively.

By comparison, gold (Au) and chromium (Cr) are unreactive. Gold is valued not only because it's rare but also because it does not react easily in air and it stays shiny. Chromium is plated on objects left outdoors, such as automobile trim, because it has very low reactivity to air and water.

The reactivities of other metals fall somewhere between those of sodium and gold. They react slowly with oxygen in the atmosphere, forming metal oxides. For example, if iron is left unprotected, its surface will slowly turn to reddish-brown rust. A metal can actually wear away as the soft metal oxide flakes off. This process of reaction and wearing away is called **corrosion.**

Figure 11 When water is dripped onto sodium metal, the reaction is explosive.

☑ *Checkpoint* *How do reactive metals behave?*

Alloys

As you learned in Chapter 1, a mixture consists of two or more substances mixed together but not chemically changed. Do metals form useful mixtures? Think about the steel in an automobile, the brass in a trumpet, and the bronze in a statue. Each of these materials is made of different metals mixed together.

A mixture of metals is called an **alloy.** Useful alloys combine the best properties of two or more metals into a single substance. For example, copper is a fairly soft and malleable metal. But mixed with tin, it forms bronze, which can be cast into statues that last hundreds of years. Brass is an alloy of copper and zinc. Pure iron rusts very easily, but when mixed with carbon, chromium, and vanadium, iron forms stainless steel. Knives and forks made of stainless steel can be washed over and over again without rusting.

Figure 12 The bronze of this statue is an alloy of copper and tin. *Classifying Is an alloy an element, compound, or mixture?*

Metals in the Periodic Table

The metals in a group, or family, have similar properties, and these family properties change gradually as you move across the table. The reactivity of the metals tends to decrease as you move from left to right across the periodic table.

Alkali Metals The metals in Group 1, from lithium to francium, are called the **alkali metals.** These metals are so reactive that they are never found uncombined in nature. In other words, they are never found as elements but only in compounds. In the laboratory, however, scientists have been able to isolate the pure, uncombined forms. As pure elements, the alkali metals are very soft and shiny. They are so soft, in fact, that you could cut them with a plastic knife!

The two most important alkali metals are sodium and potassium. Sodium compounds are found in large amounts in sea water and salt beds. Your diet includes many compounds that contain sodium and potassium, both of which are essential for life. Another alkali metal, lithium, is used in batteries and certain drugs.

Why are the alkali metals so reactive? The answer lies with their valence electrons. Each atom of an alkali metal has one valence electron that is easily transferred to other atoms during a chemical change. When that valence electron is gone, the part of the atom that remains is much more stable.

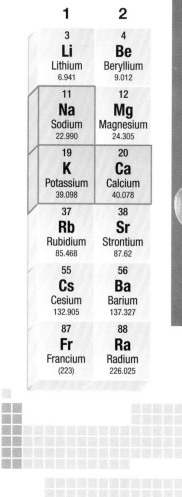

1	2
3 **Li** Lithium 6.941	4 **Be** Beryllium 9.012
11 **Na** Sodium 22.990	12 **Mg** Magnesium 24.305
19 **K** Potassium 39.098	20 **Ca** Calcium 40.078
37 **Rb** Rubidium 85.468	38 **Sr** Strontium 87.62
55 **Cs** Cesium 132.905	56 **Ba** Barium 137.327
87 **Fr** Francium (223)	88 **Ra** Radium 226.025

Figure 13 Intravenous fluids (above center) must provide elements, such as potassium and sodium, that are important to living cells. Calcium is part of the compound that makes up the limestone of these cliffs (above right). *Interpreting Diagrams To which families do the metals potassium, sodium, and calcium belong?*

Alkaline Earth Metals Group 2 of the periodic table contains the **alkaline earth metals.** While not as reactive as the metals in Group 1, these elements are more reactive than most metals. They are never found uncombined in nature. Each is fairly hard, bright white, and a good conductor of electricity.

The two most common alkaline earth metals are magnesium and calcium. Magnesium was once used in flash bulbs because it gives off a very bright light when it burns. Magnesium also combines with aluminum, making a strong but lightweight alloy. This alloy is used to make ladders, airplane parts, and other products. Calcium is an essential part of teeth and bones, and it also helps muscles work properly. You get calcium from milk and other dairy products, as well as green, leafy vegetables.

Each atom of an alkaline earth metal has two valence electrons. Like the alkali metals, the alkaline earth metals easily lose their valence electrons in chemical reactions. Each alkaline earth metal is almost as reactive as its neighbor to the left in the periodic table.

Transition Metals The elements in Groups 3 through 12 are called the **transition metals.** The transition metals form a bridge between the very reactive metals on the left side of the periodic table and the less reactive metals and other elements on the right side. The transition metals are so similar to one another that differences between nearby columns are often difficult to detect.

The transition metals include most of the familiar metals, such as iron, copper, nickel, silver, and gold. Most of the transition metals are hard and shiny. Gold, copper, and some other transition metals have unusual colors. All of the transition metals are good conductors of electricity.

The transition metals are fairly stable, reacting slowly or not at all with air and water. Ancient gold coins and jewelry are as beautiful and detailed today as they were thousands of years ago. Even when iron reacts with air and water, forming rust, it sometimes takes many years to react completely, not at all like the violent reactions of the alkali metals.

INTEGRATING LIFE SCIENCE Would you believe that you use transition metals inside your body? In fact, you would not survive very long without one of the transition metals—iron. Iron is an important part of a large molecule called hemoglobin, which carries oxygen in your bloodstream. Hemoglobin also gives blood its bright red color.

Metals in Mixed Groups Groups 13 through 16 of the periodic table include metals, nonmetals, and metalloids. The metals in these groups to the right of the transition metals are not nearly as reactive as those on the left side of the table. The most familiar of these metals are aluminum, tin, and lead. Aluminum is the lightweight metal used in beverage cans and airplane bodies. A thin layer of tin is used to coat steel to protect it from corrosion in cans of food. Lead is a shiny, blue-white metal that was once used in paints and water pipes. But lead is poisonous, so it is no longer used for these purposes. Now its most common use is in automobile batteries.

✓ *Checkpoint* *Which groups are considered transition metals?*

Figure 14 Transition metals are used to make colorful paints, including cobalt blue, zinc white, cadmium red, and chromium oxide green.

3	4	5	6	7	8	9	10	11	12
21 **Sc** Scandium 44.956	22 **Ti** Titanium 47.88	23 **V** Vanadium 50.942	24 **Cr** Chromium 51.996	25 **Mn** Manganese 54.938	26 **Fe** Iron 55.847	27 **Co** Cobalt 58.933	28 **Ni** Nickel 58.69	29 **Cu** Copper 63.546	30 **Zn** Zinc 65.39
39 **Y** Yttrium 88.906	40 **Zr** Zirconium 91.224	41 **Nb** Niobium 92.906	42 **Mo** Molybdenum 95.94	43 **Tc** Technetium (98)	44 **Ru** Ruthenium 101.07	45 **Rh** Rhodium 102.906	46 **Pd** Palladium 106.42	47 **Ag** Silver 107.868	48 **Cd** Cadmium 112.411
57 **La** Lanthanum 138.906	72 **Hf** Hafnium 178.49	73 **Ta** Tantalum 180.948	74 **W** Tungsten 183.85	75 **Re** Rhenium 186.207	76 **Os** Osmium 190.23	77 **Ir** Iridium 192.22	78 **Pt** Platinum 195.08	79 **Au** Gold 196.967	80 **Hg** Mercury 200.59
89 **Ac** Actinium 227.028	104 **Rf** Rutherfordium (261)	105 **Db** Dubnium (262)	106 **Sg** Seaborgium (263)	107 **Bh** Bohrium (262)	108 **Hs** Hassium (265)	109 **Mt** Meitnerium (266)	110 **Uun** Ununnilium (269)	111 **Uuu** Unununium (272)	112 **Uub** Ununbium (272)

58	59	60	61	62	63	64	65	66	67	68	69	70	71
Ce	Pr	Nd	Pm	Sm	Eu	Gd	Tb	Dy	Ho	Er	Tm	Yb	Lu
90	91	92	93	94	95	96	97	98	99	100	101	102	103
Th	Pa	U	Np	Pu	Am	Cm	Bk	Cf	Es	Fm	Md	No	Lr

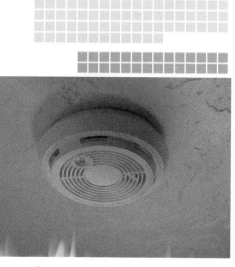

Figure 15 The actinide metal named americium is used in smoke detectors like this one.
Interpreting Diagrams What is the atomic number of americium?

Lanthanides and Actinides The elements at the bottom of the periodic table are called the **lanthanides** (LAN thuh nydz) and **actinides** (AK tuh nydz). They are also known as the rare earth elements. These elements fit in Periods 6 and 7 between the alkaline earth metals and the transition metals, but they are placed below the periodic table for convenience.

Lanthanides are soft, malleable, shiny metals with high conductivity. They are used in industry to make various alloys. Different lanthanides are usually found together in nature. They are difficult to separate from one another because all of them have very similar properties.

Of the actinides, only thorium (Th) and uranium (U) exist on Earth in any significant amounts. You may already have heard of uranium, which is used to produce energy in nuclear power plants. All of the elements after uranium in the periodic table were created artifically in laboratories. The nuclei of these elements are very unstable, meaning that they break apart very quickly into smaller nuclei. In fact, many of these synthetic elements are so unstable that they last for only a fraction of a second after they are made.

Section 2 Review

1. List four properties of most metals.
2. Compare the reactivity of metals on the left and right sides of the periodic table.
3. If you point to an element in the periodic table at random, is it more likely to be a metal, a nonmetal, or a metalloid? Explain your answer.
4. **Thinking Critically Predicting** Element 118 has not yet been made or discovered. If this element existed, however, where would it be placed in the periodic table? (*Hint:* Start at the square for element 112.) Would you expect it to be a metal, a nonmetal, or a metalloid? What properties would you predict for this element? Explain your answer.

Check Your Progress

CHAPTER PROJECT 3

Observe your samples for properties such as shininess, hardness, and color. Record these observations in your chart. Plan how to test other properties of metals such as electrical and heat conductivity, density, and reactions with acids and oxygen. Remember that you need to compare the properties of your metal samples. Have your teacher approve your experimental plan.

SCIENCE AND SOCIETY

Cleaning Up Metal Contamination

Metals are an important resource. For example, mercury is used in thermometers, medicines, and electrical equipment. Cadmium and lead are used to make batteries, and lead was used to make paints. However, these metals are poisonous, or toxic, to humans who are exposed to them over a long period of time.

Years of manufacturing have left factory buildings and the surrounding soil contaminated with toxic metals. Until 1980, no one was required to clean up property contaminated with toxic metals. Then the federal government passed the Superfund law that made landowners or previous users of properties responsible for toxic cleanups.

The Issues

Should People Clean Up and Build on Contaminated Land? About 450,000 factories, mines, and dumps in the United States have been closed because of contamination with toxic metals. One cleanup method is to scrape off the contaminated layer of soil and take it to a landfill specially constructed for hazardous wastes. Another common method is to cover the contaminated land with a thick layer of clean soil or a substance that water can't penetrate. The idea is to stop the spread of contamination.

Health experts say the worst sites should be cleaned up to keep people from being exposed to toxic metals. Or at least, sites need to be fenced off. They do not want the sites used again.

Builders, on the other hand, want to clean up the land and build new factories, offices, and houses on it. Some public officials also favor building on the land because construction provides jobs.

How Much Cleanup Is Necessary? Some people only want to clean up sites where people live. They say that contact with toxic metals in homes is more dangerous than contact in workplaces since people spend more time at home than at work. These people favor complete cleanup of building sites for homes but less complete cleanup of factory and office sites. Limiting the amount of cleanup also reduces the cost.

Other people favor a complete cleanup of all contaminated sites. Toxic metals in the soil of industrial sites could spread to nearby homes or seep into groundwater. People also might build their homes near contaminated sites in the future.

Who Is Responsible for Cleanups? Taking down contaminated buildings, removing soil, and covering sites is expensive. And, determining who is responsible for long-abandoned sites is complicated. The Superfund law, other federal laws, and laws of the individual states differ as to whether current owners or past users are responsible. For some sites, federal or state money may be required to pay for cleanups.

You Decide

1. Identify the Problem
In your own words, explain the problem of sites contaminated with toxic metals.

2. Analyze the Options
How could people benefit by building on contaminated lands? How might people be hurt?

3. Find a Solution
Suppose you are a builder, a factory worker, a landowner, or someone living next to a contaminated site. State and defend your opinion on building on that site.

Testing 1, 2, 3

What materials make the best plumbing pipes? Or the best electrical wiring? Or the best lead for a pencil? A materials scientist answers questions such as these. Materials scientists work to find the best materials for different products. To understand materials, you need to know their basic properties. In this lab, you will be comparing the properties of a copper wire and a sample of graphite. Graphite is a form of the element carbon.

Problem

How does copper compare to graphite?

Skills Focus

observing, interpreting data, classifying

Materials

1.5-V dry cell	hot plate
200-mL beaker	water
stopwatch	

flashlight bulb and socket

3 lengths of insulated wire

thin copper wire with no insulation, about 5–6 cm long

2 graphite samples (lead from a mechanical pencil), each about 5–6 cm long

Procedure

1. Fill a 200-mL beaker about three-fourths full with water. Heat it slowly on a hot plate. Let the water continue to heat as you complete Part 1 and Part 2 of the investigation.

Part 1 Physical Properties

2. Compare the shininess and color of your two samples. Record your observations.

3. Bend the copper wire as far as possible. Next, bend one of the graphite samples as far as possible. Record the results of each test.

Part 2 Electrical Conductivity

4. Place a bulb into a lamp socket. Use a piece of insulated wire to connect one pole of a dry cell battery to the socket, as shown in the photo below.

5. Attach the end of a second piece of insulated wire to the other pole of the dry cell battery. Leave the other end of this wire free.

6. Attach the end of a third piece of insulated wire to the other pole of the lamp socket. Leave the other end of this wire free.

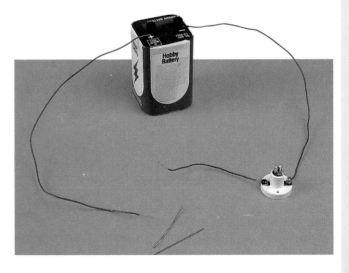

7. Touch the free ends of the insulated wire to the ends of the copper wire. Record your observations of the bulb.

8. Repeat Step 7 using a graphite sample instead of the copper wire.

Part 3 Heat Conductivity

9. Turn off the hot plate.
10. Hold one end of a graphite sample between the fingertips of one hand. Hold one end of the copper wire between the fingertips of the other hand.
11. Dip both the graphite and copper wire into the hot water at the same time. Allow only about 1 cm of each piece to reach under the water's surface. From your fingertips to the water, the lengths of both the graphite sample and the copper wire should be approximately equal.
12. Time how long it takes to feel the heat in the fingertips of each hand. Record your observations.

Analyze and Conclude

1. Compare the physical properties of copper and graphite that you observed.
2. Describe the results of the electrical conductivity and heat conductivity tests that you performed.

3. Based on the observations you made in this lab, explain why copper is classified as a metal and carbon is not classified as a metal.
4. In Step 11, why was it important to use equal lengths of copper wire and graphite?
5. **Apply** Based on your observations and conclusions from this lab, for what products might copper and graphite be best suited?

Design an Experiment

The density of metals is generally greater than the density of nonmetals. Design a procedure that would compare the density of copper and graphite. With your teacher's approval, conduct your investigation.

What Are the Properties of Charcoal?

1. Break off a piece of charcoal and roll it between your fingers. Record your observations.

2. Rub the charcoal on a piece of paper. Describe what happens.

3. Strike the charcoal sharply with the blunt end of a butter knife or fork. Describe what happens.

4. When you are finished with your investigation, return the charcoal to your teacher and wash your hands.

Think It Over

Classifying Charcoal is a form of the element carbon. Would you classify carbon as a metal or a nonmetal? Use your observations from this activity to explain your answer.

◆ Where are nonmetals and metalloids located on the periodic table?

◆ What are the properties of nonmetals and metalloids?

Reading Tip As you read about each family of nonmetals, make a list of their properties.

Think of ten objects that do not contain metal. Some of the objects might be soft and smooth, such as an animal's fur, a blade of grass, or a silk shirt. But you may have thought of objects that are much harder, such as the bark or wood of a tree or the plastic case of a computer. You might also have thought of liquids, such as water and gasoline, or gases, such as the nitrogen and oxygen gases that make up the atmosphere.

Your world is full of materials that contain little or no metal. What's more, these materials have a wide variety of properties, ranging from soft to hard, from flexible to breakable, and from solid to gaseous. To understand these properties, you need to study another important category of the elements: the nonmetals.

What Is a Nonmetal?

Nonmetals are the elements that lack most of the properties of metals. **There are 17 nonmetals, each located to the right of the zigzag line in the periodic table.** As you will discover, many of the nonmetals are very common elements, as well as extremely important to all living things on Earth.

Figure 16 Living organisms, like this raccoon and these reeds, are made up mostly of nonmetals, such as the elements carbon, hydrogen, oxygen, and nitrogen.

Physical Properties Many of the nonmetal elements are gases at room temperature, which means they have low boiling points. The air you breathe is made mostly of two nonmetals, nitrogen (N) and oxygen (O). Other nonmetal elements, such as carbon (C) and iodine (I), are solids at room temperature. Bromine (Br) is the only nonmetal that is liquid at room temperature.

In general, the physical properties of nonmetals are opposite to those that characterize the metals. Most nonmetals are dull, unlike shiny metals. Solid nonmetals are brittle, meaning they are not malleable and not ductile. If you pound on most solid nonmetals with a hammer, they break easily or crumble into a powder. Nonmetals usually have lower densities than metals. Nonmetals are also poor conductors of heat and electricity.

Figure 17 Nonmetal solids, such as this sulfur, tend to be crumbly when hit with a hammer. *Comparing and Contrasting What would you expect to happen if you hammered a metal such as copper or gold?*

Chemical Properties Most nonmetals readily form compounds. But the Group 18 elements hardly ever do. The difference has to do with valence electrons. Atoms of the Group 18 elements do not gain, lose, or share electrons. For this reason, the Group 18 elements do not react with other elements.

The rest of the nonmetals have atoms that can gain or share electrons. In either case, the atoms of these nonmetals can react with other atoms, leading to the formation of compounds.

Compounds of Nonmetals When nonmetals and metals react, valence electrons move from the metal atoms to the nonmetal atoms. Group 17 elements react easily this way. The product of a reaction between a metal and a nonmetal from Group 17 is a compound called a salt. An example of a salt is common table salt (NaCl), which is formed from sodium (Na) and chlorine (Cl). Other groups of nonmetals form compounds with metals, too. Rust is a compound made of iron and oxygen (Fe_2O_3). It's the reddish, flaky coating you might see on an old piece of steel or an iron nail.

Nonmetals can also form compounds with other nonmetals. The atoms share electrons and become bonded together into molecules. Many nonmetals even form molecules of two identical atoms, which are called **diatomic molecules.** Examples of diatomic molecules are oxygen (O_2), nitrogen (N_2), and hydrogen (H_2).

Figure 18 When a metal, such as sodium, reacts with a nonmetal, such as chlorine, a valence electron is transferred from each sodium atom to a chlorine atom. When two identical atoms of a nonmetal react, they share electrons.

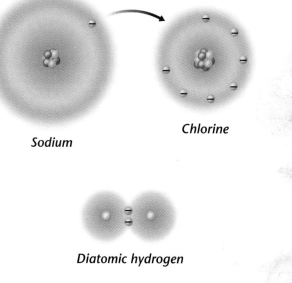

Sodium   *Chlorine*

Diatomic hydrogen

Checkpoint *In which portion of the periodic table do you find nonmetals?*

14	15
6 **C** Carbon 12.011	**7** **N** Nitrogen 14.007
14 **Si** Silicon 28.086	**15** **P** Phosphorus 30.974
32 **Ge** Germanium 72.61	**33** **As** Arsenic 74.922
50 **Sn** Tin 118.710	**51** **Sb** Antimony 121.75
82 **Pb** Lead 207.2	**83** **Bi** Bismuth 208.980

Figure 19 Charcoal (above center) is composed mostly of the element carbon. Farmers provide their growing plants with fertilizers (above right) that include the element nitrogen. *Applying Concepts Which has the greater mass, an atom of carbon or an atom of nitrogen? How can you tell?*

Families of Nonmetals

Look at the periodic table in Section 1 or in Appendix D, and notice the groups that contain nonmetals. Only Group 18 contains nonmetals exclusively. Other groups, such as Groups 14 and 15, contain three classes of elements: nonmetals, metals, and a third class of elements called metalloids. For this reason, the elements in Groups 14 and 15 are not as similar to each other as are elements in other groups.

The Carbon Family Group 14 is also known as the carbon family. Each element in the carbon family has atoms with 4 valence electrons. Only one of the elements is a nonmetal, and that element is carbon itself. (The next two elements, silicon and germanium, are metalloids. Tin and lead are metals.)

What makes carbon especially important is its role in the chemistry of life. All living things contain compounds that are made of long chains of carbon atoms. Scientists have identified millions of these compounds, some of which have carbon chains over a billion atoms long. You will learn much more about carbon and its compounds in the next chapter.

The Nitrogen Family Group 15, the nitrogen family, contains

INTEGRATING LIFE SCIENCE elements that have 5 valence electrons in their atoms. The two nonmetals in the family are nitrogen and phosphorus. To introduce yourself to nitrogen, take a deep breath. The atmosphere is almost 80 percent nitrogen gas. Nitrogen (N_2) gas does not readily react with other elements, however, so you breathe out as much nitrogen as you breathe in.

Living things do use nitrogen, but most living things are unable to use the nitrogen gas in the air. Only certain kinds of bacteria—tiny, microscopic creatures—are able to combine the nitrogen in the air with other elements, a process called nitrogen fixation. Plants can then take up the nitrogen compounds formed in the soil by the bacteria. Farmers also add nitrogen compounds to the soil in the form of fertilizers. Like all animals, you get the nitrogen you need from the food you eat—from plants, or from animals that ate plants.

Phosphorus is the other nonmetal in the nitrogen family. Unlike nitrogen, phosphorus is not stable as an element. So, phosphorus in nature is always found in compounds. The reactivity of phosphorus is one reason why it is used to make matches and flares.

☑ *Checkpoint* *What are the Group 15 elements?*

The Oxygen Family Group 16, the oxygen family, contains elements that have 6 valence electrons in their atoms. An atom in Group 16 typically gains or shares 2 electrons when it reacts. The three nonmetals in the oxygen family are oxygen, sulfur, and a rarer element named selenium.

You are using oxygen right now. With every breath, oxygen travels through your lungs and into your bloodstream, which distributes it all over your body. You could not live long without a steady supply of oxygen. The oxygen you breathe is a diatomic molecule (O_2). In addition, oxygen sometimes forms a triatomic (three-atom) molecule, which is called ozone (O_3). Ozone collects in a layer in the upper atmosphere, where it screens out harmful radiation from the sun.

Oxygen is very reactive, and can combine with almost every other element. It also is the most abundant element in Earth's crust and the second most abundant element in the atmosphere.

Sulfur is the other common nonmetal in the oxygen family. If you have ever smelled the odor of a rotten egg, then you are already familiar with the smell of many sulfur compounds. These compounds have a strong, unpleasant odor. You can also find sulfur in rubber bands, automobile tires, and many medicines.

Show Me the Oxygen

How can you test for the presence of oxygen?

1. 🧪🧤 Pour about a 3-cm depth of hydrogen peroxide (H_2O_2) into a test tube.

2. Add a pea-sized amount of manganese dioxide (MnO_2) to the test tube.

3. Observe the test tube for about 1 minute.

4. 🔥 When instructed by your teacher, set a wooden splint on fire.

5. Blow the splint out after 5 seconds and immediately plunge the glowing splint into the mouth of the test tube. Avoid getting the splint wet.

Observing Describe the change in matter that occured in the test tube. What evidence indicates that oxygen was produced?

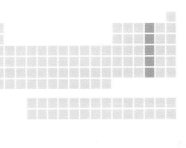

16
8
O
Oxygen
15.999
16
S
Sulfur
32.066
34
Se
Selenium
78.96
52
Te
Tellurium
127.60
84
Po
Polonium
(209)

Figure 20 The making of modern rubber depends on the element sulfur. *Interpreting Diagrams Which element is above sulfur in the periodic table?*

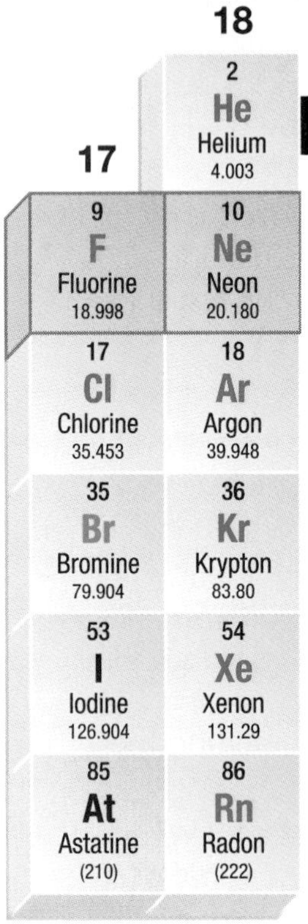

The Halogen Family Group 17 contains fluorine, chlorine, bromine, iodine, and astatine. It is also known as the **halogen family.** All but one of the halogens are nonmetals, and all share similar properties. A halogen atom has 7 valence electrons and typically gains or shares one electron when it reacts.

All of the halogens are very reactive, and most of them are dangerous to humans. But many of the compounds that halogens form are also quite useful. Fluorine, the most reactive of all the nonmetals, is found in nonstick cookware and compounds that help prevent tooth decay. Chlorine is already familiar to you in one form—ordinary table salt is a compound of sodium and chlorine. Other salts of chlorine include calcium chloride, which is used to help melt snow. Bromine reacts with silver to form silver bromide, which is used in photographic film.

The Noble Gases The elements in Group 18 are known as the **noble gases.** In some cultures, "noble" individuals held a high rank and did not work or mix with "ordinary" people. The noble gases do not ordinarily form compounds with other elements. This is because atoms of noble gases do not gain, lose, or share their valence electrons. As a result, the noble gases are chemically very stable and unreactive.

All the noble gases exist in Earth's atmosphere, but only in small amounts. Because of the stability and relative scarcity of the noble gases, most were not discovered until the late 1800s. Helium was discovered by a scientist who was studying, not the atmosphere, but the sun.

Have you made use of a noble gas? You have if you have ever purchased a floating balloon filled with helium. Noble gases are also used in glowing electric lights. These lights are commonly called neon lights, even though they are often filled with argon, xenon, or other noble gases.

Hydrogen Alone in the upper left corner of the periodic table is hydrogen. Hydrogen is the simplest element—usually each of its atoms contains only one proton and one electron. Because the chemical properties of hydrogen differ very much from those of the other elements, it really cannot be grouped into a family.

Figure 21 The halogen fluorine is found in the nonstick surface of this cookware. Fluorine is a very reactive element, unlike the noble gas neon in these brightly lit signs. *Relating Cause and Effect What makes the element neon so stable?*

18	
	2 **He** Helium 4.003
17	
9 **F** Fluorine 18.998	10 **Ne** Neon 20.180
17 **Cl** Chlorine 35.453	18 **Ar** Argon 39.948
35 **Br** Bromine 79.904	36 **Kr** Krypton 83.80
53 **I** Iodine 126.904	54 **Xe** Xenon 131.29
85 **At** Astatine (210)	86 **Rn** Radon (222)

Figure 22 The tiny atoms of the element hydrogen are very reactive.

1 **H** Hydrogen 1.008

Although hydrogen makes up more than 90 percent of the atoms in the universe, it makes up only 1.0 percent of the mass of Earth's crust, oceans, and atmosphere. Hydrogen is rarely found on Earth as a pure element. Most of it is combined with oxygen in water. If the chemical bonds in water are broken, then diatomic molecules of hydrogen (H_2) gas are formed.

✓ *Checkpoint* *Which elements are called halogens?*

The Metalloids

On the border between the metals and the nonmetals are seven elements called metalloids. The **metalloids** have some of the characteristics of metals and some of the characteristics of non-metals. The most common metalloid is silicon (Si). Silicon combines with oxygen to form a number of familiar substances, including sand, glass, and cement. You also may have encountered boron, which is used in some cleaning solutions. You would not want to encounter arsenic, which is a poison.

INTEGRATING PHYSICS **The most useful property of the metalloids is their varying ability to conduct electricity.** Whether or not a metalloid conducts electricity can depend on temperature, exposure to light, or the presence of small amounts of impurities. For this reason, metalloids such as silicon and germanium (Ge) are used to make semiconductors. **Semiconductors** are substances that under some conditions can carry electricity, like a metal, while under other conditions cannot carry electricity, like a nonmetal. Semiconductors are used to make computer chips, transistors, and lasers.

Figure 23 As this close up view shows, a silicon computer chip is so small it can fit through the eye of a needle.

Section 3 Review

1. Which elements in the periodic table are nonmetals and which are metalloids?
2. What properties identify nonmetals?
3. How do the noble gases differ from the other elements?
4. Describe an important use of metalloids.
5. **Thinking Critically Interpreting Diagrams** Find the following elements in the periodic table: iodine, xenon, selenium. What properties of these elements are indicated by their positions in the periodic table?

Science at Home

Make a survey of compounds in your home that contain halogens. Look at labels on foods, cooking ingredients, cleaning material, medicines, cosmetics, and pesticides. The presence of a halogen is often indicated by the prefixes *fluoro-, chloro-, bromo-, and iodo-*. Show your family examples of substances in your home that contain halogens and describe the properties of the halogen family.

ALIEN PERIODIC TABLE

Imagine that scientists have made radio contact with life on a distant planet. The planet is composed of many of the same elements as are found on Earth. But the inhabitants of the planet have different names and symbols for the elements. The radio transmission gave data on the known chemical and physical properties of 30 elements that belong to Groups 1, 2, 13, 14, 15, 16, 17, and 18. You need to place the elements into a blank periodic table based on these properties.

Problem

Where do the alien elements fit in the periodic table?

Materials

ruler
periodic table from text for reference

Procedure

1. Copy the blank periodic table below into your notebook.
2. Listed below are data on the chemical and physical properties of the 30 elements. Place the elements in their proper position in the blank periodic table.

   ◆ The noble gases are bombal (Bo), wobble (Wo), jeptum (J), and logon (L). Among these gases, wobble has the greatest atomic mass and bombal the least. Logon is lighter than jeptum.

   ◆ The most reactive group of metals are xtalt (X), byyou (By), chow (Ch), and quackzil (Q). Of these metals, chow has the lowest atomic mass. Quackzil is in the same period as wobble.

   ◆ Apstrom (A), vulcania (V), and kratt (Kt) are nonmetals whose atoms typically gain or share one electron. Vulcania is in the same period as quackzil and wobble.

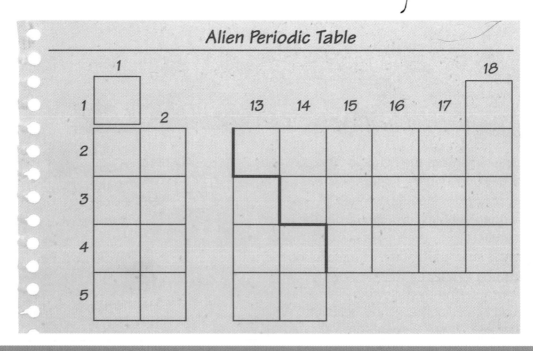

Alien Periodic Table

- The metalloids are ernst (E), highho (Hi), terriblum (T), and sississ (Ss). Sissis is the metalloid with the greatest atomic mass. Ernst is the metalloid with the lowest atomic mass. Highho and terriblum are in Group 14. Terriblum has more protons than highho. Yazzer (Yz) touches the zigzag line, but it's a metal, not a metalloid.
- The lightest element of all is called pfsst (Pf). The heaviest element in the group of 30 elements is eldorado (El). The most chemically active nonmetal is apstrom. Kratt reacts with byyou to form table salt.
- The element doggone (D) has only 4 protons in its atom.
- Floxxit (Fx) is important in the chemistry of life. It forms compounds made of long chains of atoms. Rhaatrap (R) and doadeer (Do) are metals in the fourth period, but rhaatrap is less reactive than doadeer. Magnificon (M), goldy (G), and sississ are all members of Group 15. Goldy has fewer total electrons than magnificon.
- Urrp (Up), oz (Oz), and nuutye (Nu) all gain 2 electrons when they react. Nuutye is found as a diatomic molecule and has the same properties as a gas found in Earth's atmosphere. Oz has a lower atomic number than urrp.
- The element anatom (An) has atoms with a total of 49 electrons. Zapper (Z) and pie (Pi) lose two electrons when they react. Zapper is used in flashbulbs.

Analyze and Conclude

1. List the Earth names for the 30 alien elements in order of atomic number.
2. Were you able to place some elements within the periodic table with just a single clue? Explain using examples.
3. Why did you need two or more clues to place other elements? Explain using examples.
4. Why could you use clues about atomic mass to place elements, even though the table is now based on atomic number?
5. **Think About It** Which groups of elements are not included in the alien periodic table? Do you think it is likely that an alien planet would lack these elements? Explain.

More to Explore

Notice that Period 5 is incomplete on the alien periodic table. Create names and symbols for each of the missing elements. Then, compose a series of clues that would allow another student to identify these elements. Make your clues as precise as possible.

SECTION 4 Elements From Stardust

DISCOVER ····· ACTIVITY ···

Can Helium Be Made From Hydrogen?

1. Every hydrogen atom consists of a nucleus of 1 proton surrounded by an electron. Most hydrogen nuclei do not contain neutrons, but some contain 1 or 2 neutrons. Draw models of each of the three kinds of hydrogen atoms.

2. All helium atoms have 2 protons and 2 electrons, and almost all have 2 neutrons. Draw a model of a typical helium atom.

Think it Over

Developing Hypotheses How might hydrogen atoms combine to form a helium atom? Draw a diagram to illustrate your hypothesis. Why would hydrogen nuclei with neutrons be important for this process?

GUIDE FOR READING

◆ How do new elements form inside stars?

Reading Tip Before you read, think of questions to pose about what happens inside of stars like the sun. Then read to find answers to your questions.

Have you wondered where the elements come from? Would you like to know why some elements are common here on Earth, while others are much rarer?

To answer questions such as these, scientists have looked in a place that might surprise you: the inside of stars. By studying the sun and other stars, scientists have formed some interesting hypotheses about the origins of matter here on Earth.

Atomic Nuclei Collide

Like many other stars, the sun is made mostly of one element—hydrogen. This hydrogen exists at tremendously high pressures and hot temperatures. How hot is it? The temperature in the sun's core is about 15 million degrees Celsius.

At the high pressures and hot temperatures found inside the sun and other stars, hydrogen does not exist as either a solid, liquid, or gas. Instead, it exists in a state called plasma. In the **plasma** state of matter, atoms are stripped of their electrons and the nuclei are packed close together.

Remember that atomic nuclei contain protons, which means that nuclei are positively charged. Normally, positively charged nuclei repel each other. But inside stars, where matter is in the plasma state, nuclei are close enough and moving fast enough to collide with each other.

When colliding nuclei have enough energy, they can join together in a process called nuclear fusion. In **nuclear fusion,** atomic nuclei combine to form a larger nucleus, releasing huge amounts of energy in the process. **Inside stars, nuclear fusion combines smaller nuclei into larger nuclei, thus creating heavier elements.** For this reason, you can think of stars as "element factories."

☑ *Checkpoint* *What does "nuclear fusion" mean?*

Elements From the Sun

What are the steps of nuclear fusion in the sun and other stars? To answer this question, you need to take a close look at the nuclei of hydrogen atoms. A hydrogen nucleus always contains one proton. However, different types of hydrogen nuclei can contain 2 neutrons, 1 neutron, or no neutrons at all.

Inside the sun, hydrogen nuclei undergo a nuclear fusion reaction that produces helium nuclei, as illustrated in Figure 25. Notice that the reaction requires a type of hydrogen nuclei that contains neutrons. This form of hydrogen is rare on Earth, but it is much more common inside the sun.

As two hydrogen nuclei fuse together, they release a great deal of energy. In fact, this reaction is the major source of the energy that the sun now produces. In other words, hydrogen is the fuel that powers the sun. Although the sun will eventually run out of hydrogen, scientists estimate that the sun has enough hydrogen to last another 5 billion years.

As more and more helium builds up in the core, the sun's temperature and volume also change. These changes allow different nuclear fusion reactions to occur. Over time, two or more helium nuclei combine to form the nuclei of slightly heavier elements. First, two helium nuclei combine, forming a beryllium nucleus. Then, another helium nucleus can join with the beryllium nucleus, forming a carbon nucleus. And yet another helium

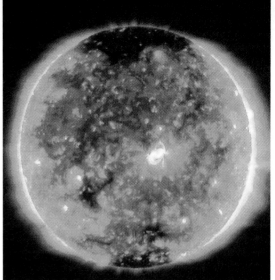

Figure 24 Without the nuclear fusion inside the sun, no sunlight would reach Earth. *Predicting What might happen in 5 billion years when all the hydrogen in the sun's core is used up?*

Figure 25 In the process of nuclear fusion, hydrogen nuclei combine, producing helium and tremendous amounts of energy.

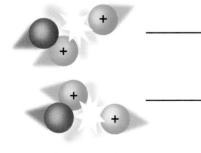
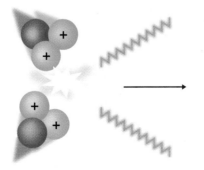

Hydrogen nuclei (with and without neutrons)

Helium nuclei (one neutron each)

Helium nucleus

Hydrogen nuclei

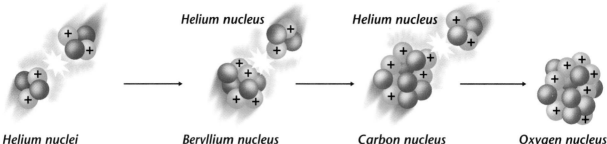

Helium nucleus   Helium nucleus

Helium nuclei   Beryllium nucleus   Carbon nucleus   Oxygen nucleus

Figure 26 A series of nuclear fusion reactions forms nuclei larger than helium. *Interpreting Diagrams Which elements are being formed?*

nucleus can join with the carbon nucleus, forming oxygen. But stars the size of the sun do not contain enough energy to produce elements heavier than oxygen.

Elements From Large Stars

As they age, larger stars become even hotter than the sun. These stars have enough energy to produce heavier elements, such as magnesium and silicon. In more massive stars, fusion continues until the core is almost all iron.

How are elements heavier than iron produced? In the final hours of the most massive stars, scientists have observed an event called a supernova. A **supernova** is a tremendous explosion that breaks apart a massive star, producing temperatures up to one billion degrees Celsius. A supernova provides enough energy for the nuclear fusion reactions that create the heaviest elements.

Most astronomers agree that the matter in the sun and the planets around it, including Earth, originally came from a gigantic supernova that occurred billions of years ago. If this is true, it means that everything around you was created in a star. So all matter on Earth is a form of stardust.

Figure 27 When massive stars explode in a supernova, enough energy is released to form the heavier elements.

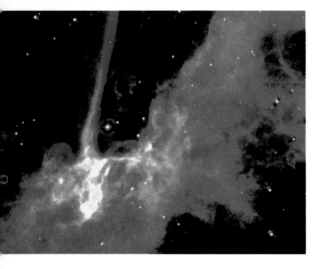

Section 4 Review

1. How does nuclear fusion produce new elements?
2. What nuclear fusion reaction occurs in stars like the sun?
3. How do the fusion reactions in the sun compare to the fusion occurring in larger stars and supernovas?
4. **Thinking Critically Inferring** Plasma is not found naturally on Earth. Why do you think this is so?

Check Your Progress

CHAPTER PROJECT
3

With your teacher's approval, begin testing the metal samples. Record the results of each test. If you cannot measure a property with exact numbers, use a more general rating system. For example, you could describe each metal as showing a particular property very well, somewhat, poorly, or not at all.

SECTION 1 Organizing the Elements

Key Ideas

◆ Mendeleev developed the first periodic table of the elements. An element's properties can be predicted from its location in the periodic table.

◆ Each square of the periodic table contains information about one element, often including its atomic number, chemical symbol, name, and atomic mass.

◆ The main body of the periodic table is arranged into 18 columns, called groups, and 7 rows, called periods.

◆ The properties of each element can be predicted from its location in the periodic table.

Key Terms

atomic mass	atomic number
periodic table	chemical symbol
nucleus	group
proton	family
neutron	period
electron	valence electron
atomic mass unit (amu)	

SECTION 2 Metals

Key Ideas

◆ Most of the elements are metals. Metals are found to the left of the zigzag line in the periodic table.

◆ The reactivity of metals tends to decrease as you move from left to right across the periodic table.

Key Terms

malleable	alloy
ductile	alkali metal
conductor	alkaline earth metal
magnetic	transition metal
reactivity	lanthanide
corrosion	actinide

SECTION 3 Nonmetals and Metalloids

Key Ideas

◆ There are 17 nonmetals, each located to the right of the zigzag line in the periodic table.

◆ Nonmetals lack the characteristic properties of metals. Nonmetals are dull, brittle, and poor conductors. Nonmetals can react with metals or other nonmetals.

◆ On the border between the metals and nonmetals are 7 elements called metalloids. The metalloids have some characteristics of both metals and nonmetals.

Key Terms

nonmetal	noble gas
diatomic molecule	metalloid
halogen family	semiconductor

SECTION 4 Elements From Stardust

INTEGRATING SPACE SCIENCE

Key Ideas

◆ Inside stars, nuclear fusion produces the nuclei of different elements.

◆ In stars such as the sun, hydrogen nuclei combine, forming a helium nucleus. Over time, other nuclear fusion reactions produce the nuclei of beryllium, carbon, and oxygen.

◆ Elements heavier than iron are produced in a supernova, the explosion of a very massive star.

Key Terms

plasma	nuclear fusion	supernova

USING THE INTERNET

ACTIVITY

www.science-explorer.phschool.com

Reviewing Content

For more review of key concepts, see the Interactive Student Tutorial CD-ROM.

Multiple Choice

Choose the letter of the answer that best completes the statement or answers the question.

1. In the current periodic table, elements are arranged according to
   a. atomic mass.
   b. atomic number.
   c. their bonding power with oxygen.
   d. the number of neutrons in their nuclei.
2. A horizontal row of the periodic table is called a
   a. period.　　　　b. family.
   c. group.　　　　d. noble gas.
3. Of the following, the group which contains the most reactive elements is
   a. alkali metals.
   b. alkaline earth metals.
   c. transition metals.
   d. noble gases.
4. Unlike metals, many nonmetals are
   a. good conductors of heat and electricity.
   b. malleable and ductile.
   c. gases at room temperature.
   d. shiny.
5. Inside the sun, nuclear fusion creates helium nuclei from
   a. oxygen nuclei.　　b. neon nuclei.
   c. carbon nuclei.　　d. hydrogen nuclei.

True or False

If the statement is true, write true. If it is false, change the underlined word or words to make it a true statement.

6. Dmitri Mendeleev is credited with developing the first <u>periodic table</u>.
7. The halogens are an example of a family of <u>metals</u>.
8. The <u>alkali metals</u> include iron, copper, silver, and gold.
9. Noble gases usually exist as <u>compounds</u>.
10. At the hot temperatures of stars, electrons are stripped away from nuclei. This forms a dense phase of matter called a <u>gas</u>.

Checking Concepts

11. Why did Mendeleev leave three blank spaces in his periodic table? How did he account for the blank spaces?
12. Why do elements in a group of the periodic table have similar properties?
13. List five different metals. Give examples of how each metal is used.
14. List five different nonmetals. Give examples of how each nonmetal is used.
15. Why would you expect to find the element argon in its pure, uncombined form in nature?
16. **Writing to Learn** Imagine that you are Dmitri Mendeleev, and you have just published the first periodic table. Write a letter to a fellow scientist describing the table and its value.

Thinking Visually

17. **Concept Map** Copy the concept map about the periodic table onto a separate sheet of paper. Then complete it and add a title. (For more on concept maps, see the Skills Handbook.)

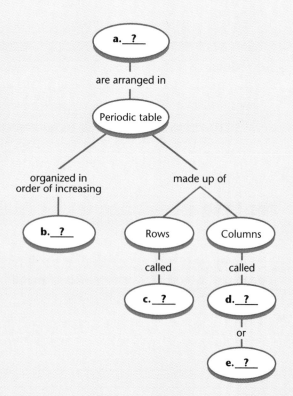

Applying Skills

The table at the right lists properties of five elements. Use the information to answer Questions 18–20.

18. **Classifying** Classify each element in the table as a metal or nonmetal. Explain your answers.
19. **Inferring** Both elements B and C have an atomic mass that is close to 40. Why can two different elements have very similar atomic masses?
20. **Drawing Conclusions** Use the periodic table to identify the five elements.

Thinking Critically

21. **Interpreting Diagrams** An atom contains 74 protons, 74 electrons, and 108 neutrons. Which element is it?
22. **Comparing and Contrasting** Compare and contrast the metals, non-metals, and metalloids. Include at least two examples of each class of elements.

Properties of Five Elements			
Element	Appearance	Atomic Mass	Conducts Electricity
A	Invisible gas	14.0	No
B	Invisible gas	39.9	No
C	Hard, silvery solid	40.0	Yes
D	Silvery liquid	200.6	Yes
E	Shiny, bluish-white solid	207.2	Slightly

23. **Drawing Conclusions** A chemistry student claims to have isolated a new element. The student states that the new element has properties similar to fluorine and chlorine, and he argues that it should be placed between fluorine and chlorine in the periodic table. Could the student have discovered a new element? Explain.
24. **Making Models** Draw a model of a carbon nucleus (6 protons, 6 neutrons) fusing with a helium nucleus (2 protons, 2 neutrons). Assuming all the protons and neutrons combine into the new nucleus, what is the identity of the new element?

Performance Assessment

CHAPTER PROJECT 3 **Wrap Up**

Presenting Your Project Display your chart that compares and contrasts the metals you studied. Be prepared to discuss which properties are common to all metals and which properties are shown by only some metals. Try to guess the types of questions that your teacher or other students might ask you.

Reflect and Record In your journal, write about other properties of metals that you could not test. Think of a set of properties that you would need to test to be able to determine if an unknown element is a metal.

Getting Involved

In Your Community Scan your local newspaper for the names of the elements. Read the articles or advertisements in which an element is mentioned.

Are any elements of special concern in your community? If so, explain why. Are some elements presented positively, while others are presented negatively? Have the names of some elements acquired other meanings?

WHAT'S AHEAD

Check Out the Fine Print

When you look at a bottle of milk, do you think about a mixture of compounds? Probably not. But all substances—the milk as well as its plastic bottle—are made of chemicals. The milk and its bottle even have something in common chemically. The plastic and many of the compounds in milk contain the element carbon. In fact, all the foods you eat and drink contain carbon compounds. In this project, you will look closely at the labels on various food packages to find carbon compounds.

Your Goal To identify carbon compounds found in different foods.

To complete the project you must
- ◆ collect at least a dozen labels with lists of ingredients and nutrition facts
- ◆ identify the carbon compounds listed, as well as substances that do not contain carbon
- ◆ interpret the nutrition facts on labels to compare amounts of substances in each food
- ◆ classify compounds in foods into the categories of polymers found in living things

Get Started Brainstorm with your classmates about what kinds of packaged foods you want to examine. For which types of food will it be easy to obtain nutrition labels?

Check Your Progress You'll be working on this project as you study this chapter. To keep your project on track, look for Check Your Progress boxes at the following points.

Section 1 Review, page 115: Collect food labels and locate nutrition facts.

Section 3 Review, page 133: Identify and classify compounds found in foods.

Wrap Up At the end of the chapter (page 139), you will present a chart of your findings about the chemicals in foods.

Both the plastic bottles in this bottling plant and the milk in them include carbon compounds.

SECTION 1 Chemical Bonding, Carbon Style

DISCOVER · ACTIVITY · · · ·

Why Do Pencils Write?

1. Tear paper into pieces about 5 cm by 5 cm. Rub two pieces back and forth between your fingers.

2. Now rub pencil lead (graphite) on one side of each piece of paper. Try to get as much graphite as possible on the paper.

3. Rub the two pieces of paper together with the sides covered with graphite touching.

4. When you are finished, wash your hands.

Think It Over

Observing Did you notice a difference in what you observed in Step 1 and Step 3? How could the property of graphite you observed be used for purposes other than pencil lead?

GUIDE FOR READING

◆ Why can carbon form a huge variety of different compounds?

◆ What are the different forms of pure carbon?

Reading Tip Before you read, list characteristics of the element carbon you already know. Add to your list as you read.

O pen your mouth and say "aah." Uh-oh, you have a small cavity. Do you know what happens next? Your tooth needs a filling. But first the dentist's drill clears away the decayed part of your tooth.

Why is a dentist's drill hard and sharp enough to cut through teeth? The answer begins with the element carbon. The tip of the drill is made of diamond—a form of carbon and the hardest substance on Earth. Because it has a diamond tip, a dentist's drill stays sharp and useful. To understand why diamond is such a hard substance, you need to take a close look at the carbon atom and the bonds it forms.

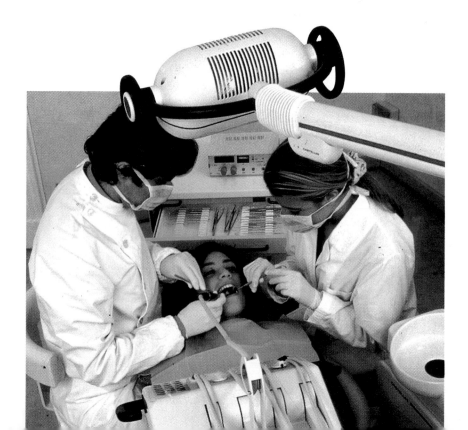

Figure 1 The tip of a dentist's drill is made of diamond, a form of carbon.

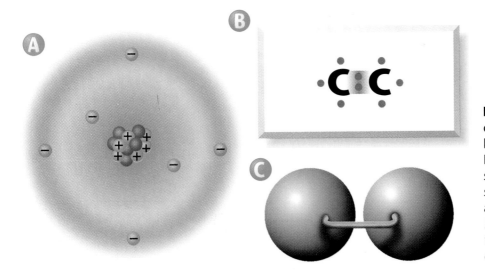

Figure 2 The atomic number of carbon is 6. **A.** Each carbon atom has four valence electrons. **B.** The valence electrons can be shown as dots around the chemical symbols. **C.** A bond hooks two atoms together.
Interpreting Diagrams How many valence electrons are involved in one bond?

The Carbon Atom and Its Bonds

Recall that the atomic number of carbon is 6. This means that the nucleus of a carbon atom contains 6 protons. Surrounding the nucleus are 6 electrons. Of these electrons, four are valence electrons—the electrons available for bonding.

As you have learned, a chemical bond is the force that holds two atoms together. You can think of the two atoms as hooked together. A chemical bond between two atoms is made up of the atoms' valence electrons. Two atoms gain, lose, or share valence electrons in the way that makes the atoms most stable. The transfer or sharing of valence electrons creates chemical bonds.

Atoms of all elements (except the noble gases) form chemical bonds. **But few elements have the ability of carbon to bond with both itself and other elements in so many different ways.**

Carbon atoms form more bonds than most other atoms. With four valence electrons, each carbon atom is able to form four bonds. In comparison, hydrogen, oxygen, and nitrogen can only form one, two, or three bonds. With four bonds to each carbon, it is possible to form substances with many carbon atoms, even thousands of them.

As you can see in Figure 3, it is possible to arrange the same number of carbon atoms in different ways. Carbon atoms can form straight chains, branched chains, and rings. Sometimes even networks of two or more rings of carbon atoms are joined together.

Figure 3 These carbon chains and rings form the backbones for molecules. In these molecules, atoms of other elements are bonded to the carbons.

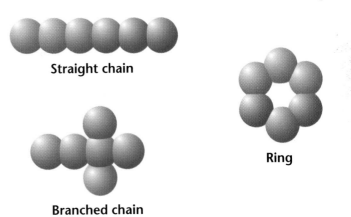

Straight chain

Branched chain

Ring

☑ *Checkpoint* How many bonds can a carbon atom form?

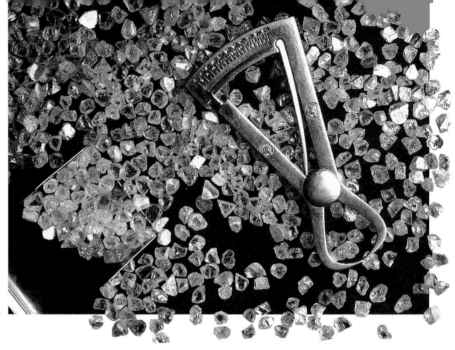

Figure 4 The carbon atoms in a diamond are arranged in a crystal structure. The diamonds in this photo have not yet been cut and polished by a jeweler.

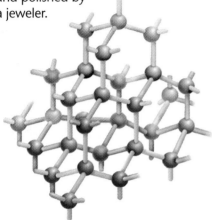

Figure 5 The carbon atoms in graphite are arranged in layers. You use graphite every time you write with a pencil.
Applying Concepts How can you explain the slipperiness of graphite?

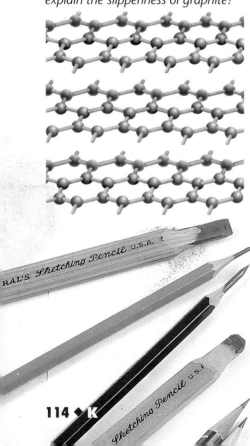

Forms of Pure Carbon

Because of the ways carbon forms bonds, the pure element can exist in different forms. **Diamond, graphite, and fullerene are three forms of the element carbon.**

Diamond The hardest mineral—**diamond**—forms deep within

![INTEGRATING EARTH SCIENCE]

Earth. At very high temperatures and pressures, carbon atoms form diamond crystals. Each carbon atom is bonded strongly to four other carbon atoms. The result is a solid that is extremely hard and unreactive. The melting point of diamond is over 3,500°C. That's as hot as the surface temperatures of some stars.

Diamonds are prized for their brilliance and clarity when cut as gems. They can have color if there are traces of other elements in the crystals. Industrial chemists are able to make diamonds artificially, but these diamonds are not beautiful enough to use as gems. Like many natural diamonds, artificial ones are used only in industry. Diamonds work well in cutting tools, such as drills.

Graphite Every time you write with a pencil, you leave a layer of carbon on the paper. The "lead" in a lead pencil is actually **graphite,** another form of the element carbon. It does not contain any of the element lead. In graphite, carbon atoms are bonded strongly together in flat layers. However, the bonds connecting the layers are very weak, so the layers slide past one another easily.

Run your fingers over pencil marks, and you can feel how slippery graphite is. If you did the Discover activity, you have observed this property. Because it is so slippery, graphite makes an excellent lubricant in machines. Graphite reduces friction between the moving parts. In your home, you might use a graphite spray to help a key work better in a sticky lock.

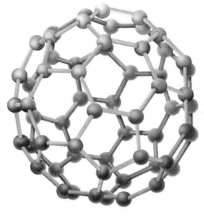

Figure 6 The arrangement of the carbon atoms in fullerenes resembles the structure of a geodesic dome or the pattern on a soccer ball.

Fullerenes In 1985, scientists at Rice University in Texas made a third form of the element carbon, a form that no one had identified before. The new form of carbon consists of carbon atoms arranged in a repeating pattern similar to the surface of a soccer ball. This form is called buckminsterfullerene, or **fullerene** (FUL ur een) for short, in honor of the architect Buckminster Fuller. Fuller designed dome-shaped buildings, called geodesic domes, which the fullerene resembles. Because of their shape, fullerenes have been given the nickname "buckyballs."

Chemists are looking for ways to use fullerenes. Because fullerenes enclose a ball-shaped open area, they may be able to carry substances inside them. Someday, fullerenes may be used to carry medicines through the body or to house very tiny computer circuits.

Section 1 Review

1. How do carbon's bonds allow the element to form so many different compounds?
2. List three different forms of pure carbon.
3. What happens to valence electrons when a chemical bond forms between atoms?
4. **Thinking Critically Comparing and Contrasting** How can you use differences in carbon bonds to explain why graphite and diamonds have different properties?

Check Your Progress

CHAPTER PROJECT 4

Collect at least one dozen food labels. Choose foods that come in clearly labeled cans, boxes, and bottles. Each label lists ingredients in order of decreasing amount. On each label, locate the table of nutrition facts. These tables list amounts of nutrients per serving and tell what percent daily nutrient needs are supplied by a serving.

HOW MANY MOLECULES?

Carbon atoms are found in an amazing variety of compounds. Some carbon compounds have just a few carbon atoms in each molecule; others have thousands. In this lab you will use gumdrops to represent atoms and toothpicks to represent bonds.

Problem

How many different ways can you put the same number of carbon atoms together?

Materials

48 toothpicks
Three colors of gumdrops:
  36 of one color
  15 of a second color
  4 or 5 of a third color (optional)

Procedure

1. You will need gumdrops of one color to represent carbon atoms and gumdrops of another color to represent hydrogen atoms. When building your models, always follow these rules:
   ◆ Each carbon atom forms four bonds.
   ◆ Each hydrogen atom forms one bond.
2. Make a model of CH_4 (methane).
3. Now make a model of C_2H_6 (ethane).

4. Make a model of C_3H_8 (propane). Is there more than one way to arrange the atoms in propane? (*Hint:* Are there any branches in the carbon chain or are all the carbon atoms in one line?)
5. Now make a model of C_4H_{10} (butane) in which all the carbon atoms are in one line.
6. Make a second model of butane with a branched chain.
7. Compare the branched-chain model with the straight-chain model of butane. Are there other ways to arrange the atoms?
8. Predict how many different structures can be formed from C_5H_{12} (pentane).
9. Test your prediction by building as many different models of pentane as you can.

Analyze and Conclude

1. Did any of your models have a hydrogen atom between two carbon atoms? Why or why not?
2. How does a branched chain differ from a straight chain?
3. How many different structures have the formula C_3H_8? C_4H_{10}? C_5H_{12}? Use diagrams to explain your answer.
4. If you bend a straight chain of carbons, do you make a different structure? Why or why not?
5. **Think About It** Compare the information you can get from models to the information you can get from formulas like C_6H_{14}. How does using models help you understand the structure of a molecule?

More to Explore

Use a third color of gumdrops to model an oxygen atom. An oxygen atom forms two bonds. Use the rules in this lab to model as many different structures for the formula $C_4H_{10}O$ as possible.

② Carbon Compounds

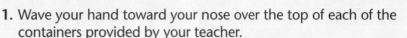

What Do You Smell?

1. Wave your hand toward your nose over the top of each of the containers provided by your teacher.

2. Try to identify each of the odors.

3. After you record what you think is in each container, compare your guesses to the actual substance.

Think It Over
Developing Hypotheses Make a hypothesis to explain the differences between the smell of one substance and the smell of another.

Imagine that you are heading out for a day of shopping. Your first purchase is a red cotton shirt. Then you go to the drug store, where you buy a bottle of shampoo and a tablet of writing paper. Your next stop is a hardware store to buy propane, a fuel used in camping stoves and lanterns. Your final stop is the grocery store, where you buy cereal, meat, and vegetables.

What do all of these purchases have in common? They all are made of carbon compounds. Carbon atoms act as the backbone or skeleton for the molecules of these compounds. Carbon compounds include gases (such as propane), liquids (such as olive oil), and solids (such as wax and cotton). Mixtures of carbon compounds are found in foods, paper, and shampoo. In fact, more than 90 percent of all known compounds contain carbon.

GUIDE FOR READING

◆ What properties do many organic compounds have in common?

◆ What kinds of carbon chains are found in hydrocarbons?

◆ What are some examples of substituted hydrocarbons?

Reading Tip Before you read, use the headings to make an outline of the different categories of organic compounds. As you read, add information to your outline.

Organic Compounds

Carbon compounds are so numerous that they are given a special name. With some exceptions, a compound that contains carbon is called an **organic compound.** The word *organic* means "of living things." Scientists once believed that organic compounds could be produced only by living

Figure 7 Did you know that when you buy a shirt you are buying carbon compounds?

Figure 8 All living things contain organic compounds. Organic compounds include the oils used to fry foods, the plastic wrap and foam tray in which these apples are packaged, and even the apples themselves. *Inferring What does the dog have in common with the cooking oil, apples, plastic wrap, and tray?*

organisms. Organic compounds are indeed part of the solid matter of every living thing on Earth. Products made from living things, such as paper made from the wood of trees, are also organic compounds. However, organic compounds can be produced artificially. For example, plastics, fuels, cleaning solutions, and many other such products are organic compounds. The raw materials for most synthetic organic compounds come from petroleum, or crude oil.

Many organic compounds have similar properties—for example, low melting points and low boiling points. As a result, many organic compounds are liquids or gases at room temperature. Organic liquids generally have strong odors. They also do not conduct electric currents. Many organic compounds do not dissolve well in water. You may have seen the vegetable oil, which is a mixture of organic compounds, form a separate layer in a bottle of salad dressing.

Hydrocarbons

Scientists classify organic compounds into different categories. The simplest organic compounds are the hydrocarbons. A **hydrocarbon** (hy droh KAHR bun) is a compound that contains only the elements carbon and hydrogen. **The carbon chains in a hydrocarbon may be straight, branched, or ring-shaped.**

You might already recognize several common hydrocarbons. Methane, also known as natural gas, is used to heat homes. Propane is used in portable stoves and gas grills and to provide heat for hot-air balloons. Butane is the fuel in most lighters. Gasoline is a mixture of several different hydrocarbons. And paraffin wax is a hydrocarbon that is used to make candles.

Properties of Hydrocarbons All hydrocarbons are flammable, which means that they burn easily. When hydrocarbons burn, they release a great deal of energy. This is why they are used as fuels to power stoves and heaters, as well as cars, buses, and airplanes.

Like most other organic compounds, hydrocarbons mix poorly with water. Have you ever been at a gas station during a rain storm? If so, you may have noticed a thin rainbow-colored film of gasoline or oil floating on a puddle.

Formulas of Hydrocarbons Hydrocarbon compounds differ in the number of carbon and hydrogen atoms in each molecule. You can show how many atoms there are of the elements that make up each molecule of a compound by writing a formula. A **molecular formula** includes the chemical symbols of the elements in each molecule of a compound, as well as the number of atoms of each element.

The simplest hydrocarbon is methane. Its molecular formula is CH_4. The number 4 indicates the number of hydrogen atoms (H). Notice that the 4 is a subscript. **Subscripts** are written lower and smaller than the letter symbols of the elements. Notice that the symbol for carbon (C) in the formula is written without a subscript. This means that there is 1 carbon atom in the molecule.

The hydrocarbon with two carbon atoms is ethane. The formula for ethane is C_2H_6. The subscripts in this formula show that an ethane molecule is made of 2 carbon atoms and 6 hydrogen atoms. The hydrocarbon with three carbon atoms is propane (C_3H_8). How many hydrogen atoms does the subscript indicate? If you answered 8, you are right.

☑ *Checkpoint* What is a hydrocarbon?

Dry or Wet? ACTIVITY

Petroleum jelly is manufactured from hydrocarbons.

1. Carefully coat one of your fingers in petroleum jelly.
2. Dip that finger in water. Also dip a finger on your other hand in water.
3. Inspect the two fingers, and note how they feel.
4. Use a paper towel to remove the petroleum jelly, and then wash your hands thoroughly.

Inferring Compare how your two fingers looked and felt in Steps 2 and 3. What property of organic compounds does this activity demonstrate?

Figure 9 The natural gas burning at the top of this oil well is composed of hydrocarbons.

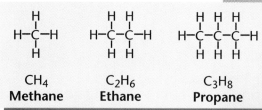

CH₄
Methane

C₂H₆
Ethane

C₃H₈
Propane

Figure 10 Each carbon atom in these structural formulas is surrounded by four dashes corresponding to four bonds. Each molecule of the propane used as the fuel in this lantern has 3 carbon atoms.

Straight Chains and Branches

If a hydrocarbon has two or more carbons, the carbon atoms can form a single line, or a straight chain. In hydrocarbons with four or more carbons, it is also possible to have branched arrangements of the carbon atoms.

Structural Formula To show how atoms are arranged in the molecules of a compound, chemists use a structural formula. A **structural formula** shows the kind, number, and arrangement of atoms in a molecule. Figure 10 shows the structural formulas for molecules of methane, ethane, and propane. Each dash (—) represents a bond. In methane, each carbon is bonded to four hydrogen atoms. In ethane and propane, each carbon is bonded to at least one carbon atom as well as to hydrogen atoms. As you look at structural formulas, notice that every carbon atom forms four bonds. Every hydrogen atom forms one bond. There are never any dangling bonds—no dangling dashes.

Figure 11 C₄H₁₀ has two isomers, butane and isobutane.
Interpreting Diagrams Which isomer is a branched chain?

Isomers Consider the molecular formula of butane—C₄H₁₀. This formula does not indicate how the atoms are arranged in a molecule. In fact, there are two different ways to arrange the carbon atoms in C₄H₁₀. These two arrangements are shown in Figure 11. Compounds that have the same molecular formula but different structures are called **isomers** (EYE soh murz). Each isomer is a different substance with its own characteristic properties.

Notice in Figure 11 that a molecule of one isomer, butane, is a straight chain. A molecule of the other isomer, isobutane, is a branched chain. Both molecules have 4 carbon atoms and 10 hydrogen atoms, but the atoms are arranged differently. And these two compounds have different properties. For example, butane and isobutane have very different melting points and boiling points.

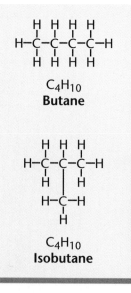

C₄H₁₀
Butane

C₄H₁₀
Isobutane

☑ Checkpoint How do structural and molecular formulas differ?

Double Bonds and Triple Bonds

So far in this section, structural formulas have shown only single bonds between any two carbon atoms. One bond, one dash. However, two carbon atoms can form a single bond, a double bond, or a triple bond. A carbon atom can also form a single or double bond with an oxygen atom. Structural formulas represent a double bond with a double dash (C=C). You might think of the two atoms as doubly hooked together. A triple bond is indicated by a triple dash (C≡C). Bonds beyond triple bonds are not found in nature.

Saturated and Unsaturated Hydrocarbons

Hydrocarbons can be classified according to the types of bonds between the carbon atoms. If a hydrocarbon has only single bonds, it has the maximum number of hydrogen atoms possible on its carbon chain. These hydrocarbons are called **saturated hydrocarbons.** You can think of each carbon as being "saturated," or filled up, with hydrogens. Hydrocarbons with double or triple bonds have fewer hydrogen atoms for each carbon atom than a saturated hydrocarbon does. They are called **unsaturated hydrocarbons.**

Notice that the names of methane, ethane, propane, and butane end with the suffix -ane. Any hydrocarbon with a name that ends in -ane is a saturated hydrocarbon. If the name of a hydrocarbon ends in -ene or -yne, it is unsaturated.

The simplest unsaturated hydrocarbon with one double bond is ethene (C_2H_4). Many fruits, such as bananas, produce ethene gas. Ethene gas helps the fruit to ripen.

The simplest hydrocarbon with one triple bond is ethyne (C_2H_2), which is commonly known as acetylene. Acetylene torches are used in welding.

Sharpen your Skills

Classifying  ACTIVITY

Which of the following hydrocarbons contain single, double, or triple bonds? (*Hint:* Remember that carbon forms four bonds and hydrogen forms one bond.)

C_2H_6	C_2H_4
C_2H_2	C_3H_8
C_3H_6	C_3H_4
C_4H_{10}	

Figure 12 Unsaturated hydrocarbons have double and triple bonds. Ethene gas causes fruits such as bananas to ripen (left). Acetylene is the fuel in the torch used for welding an oil pipeline (right).

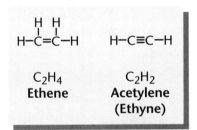

C_2H_4
Ethene

C_2H_2
Acetylene (Ethyne)

Substituted Hydrocarbons

Hydrocarbons contain only carbon and hydrogen. But carbon can form strong, stable bonds with several other elements, including oxygen, nitrogen, sulfur, and members of the halogen family. If just one atom of another element is substituted for a hydrogen atom in a hydrocarbon, a different compound is created. Such compounds are called substituted hydrocarbons. In a **substituted hydrocarbon,** atoms of other elements replace one or more hydrogen atoms in a hydrocarbon. **Substituted hydrocarbons include halogen compounds, alcohols, and organic acids.**

Halogen Compounds In some substituted hydrocarbons, one or more halogen atoms replace hydrogen atoms. Recall that the halogen family includes fluorine, chlorine, bromine, and iodine.

One halogen compound, Freon (CCl_2F_2), was widely used as a cooling liquid in refrigerators and air conditioners. When Freon was found to damage the environment, its use was banned. Safer compounds have taken Freon's place. Two halogen compounds are still used in dry cleaning solutions—trichloroethane ($C_2H_3Cl_3$) and perchloroethylene ($C_2H_2Cl_2$).

Alcohols The group –OH can also substitute for hydrogen atoms in a hydrocarbon. Each –OH, made of an oxygen atom and a hydrogen atom, is called a **hydroxyl group** (hy DRAHKS il). An **alcohol** is a substituted hydrocarbon that contains one or more hydroxyl groups.

Most alcohols dissolve well in water. They also have higher boiling points than hydrocarbons of similar size. This is why the hydrocarbon methane (CH_4) is a gas at room temperature, while the alcohol methanol (CH_3OH) is a liquid. Methanol is used to make plastics and synthetic fibers. It is also used in solutions that remove ice from airplanes. Methanol is very poisonous.

When a hydroxyl group is substituted for one hydrogen atom in ethane, the resulting alcohol is ethanol (C_2H_5OH). Ethanol is produced naturally by the action of yeast or bacteria on the sugar stored in corn, wheat, and barley. Ethanol is a good solvent for many organic compounds that do not dissolve in water. It is also added to

Figure 13 Methanol is used for de-icing an airplane in a snowstorm.
Classifying What makes methanol a substituted hydrocarbon?

H
|
H–C–OH
|
H

CH₃OH
Methanol

$$\overset{O}{\overset{\|}{H-C-OH}}$$

HCOOH
Formic acid

Figure 14 Formic acid is the simplest organic acid. It is the acid produced by ants and is reponsible for the pain caused by an ant bite.

gasoline to make a fuel for car engines called "gasohol." Ethanol is used in medicines and found in alcoholic beverages.

The ethanol used for industrial purposes is unsafe to drink. Poisonous compounds such as methanol have been added. The resulting poisonous mixture is called denatured alcohol.

Organic Acids Bite into a lemon, orange, or grapefruit. These fruits taste a little tart or sour, don't they? The sour taste of many fruits comes from citric acid, an organic acid. An **organic acid** is a substituted hydrocarbon that contains one or more of the following group of atoms: –COOH. Each –COOH is called a **carboxyl group** (kahr BAHKS il).

You can find organic acids in many foods. Acetic acid (CH_3COOH) is the main ingredient of vinegar. Malic acid is found in apples. Butyric acid makes butter smell rancid.

Stinging nettle plants make formic acid (HCOOH), the compound that makes the plant sting! The pain from ant bites also comes from formic acid.

Figure 15 Esters are responsible for the pleasant aroma and flavor of this strawberry shake.

Esters

If an alcohol and an organic acid are chemically combined, the resulting compound is called an **ester.** Many esters have pleasant, fruity smells. If you have eaten wintergreen candy, then you are familiar with the smell of an ester. Esters are also responsible for the smells of pineapples, bananas, strawberries, and apples. If you did the Discover activity, you smelled different esters. Other esters are ingredients in medications, including aspirin and the Novocaine used by dentists.

✓ *Checkpoint* *What atoms are in a carboxyl group?*

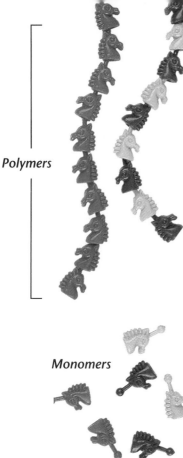

Polymers

Monomers

Figure 16 Chains of monomers that make up polymer molecules are somewhat like these chains of plastic beads. Natural polymers include the wool being sheared from this sheep.
Comparing and Contrasting How do polymer molecules differ from monomer molecules?

Polymers

Organic compounds, such as alcohols, esters, and others, can be linked together to build huge molecules with thousands or even millions of atoms. A very large molecule made of a chain of many smaller molecules bonded together is called a **polymer** (PAHL ih mur). The smaller molecules—the links that make up the chain—are called **monomers** (MAHN ih mur) The prefix *poly-* means "many," and the prefix *mono-* means "one."

Some polymers are made naturally by living things. For example, sheep make wool, cotton plants make cotton, and silk-worms make silk. In Section 3, you will learn about natural polymers that you eat. Other polymers, called **synthetic** polymers, are manufactured, or synthesized, in factories. If you are wearing clothing made from polyester or nylon, you are wearing a synthetic polymer right now! And any plastic item you use is most certainly made of synthetic polymers.

Section 2 Review

1. List properties common to many organic compounds.
2. Describe the different kinds of carbon chains that are found in hydrocarbons.
3. What is a substituted hydrocarbon? List four examples of substituted hydrocarbons.
4. **Thinking Critically Problem Solving** You are given two solid materials, one that is organic and one that is not organic. Describe three tests you could perform to help you decide which is which.

Science at Home

You can make a simple salad dressing to demonstrate one property of organic compounds. In a transparent container, thoroughly mix equal amounts of a vegetable oil and a fruit juice. Stop mixing, and observe the oil and juice mixture for several minutes. Explain your observations to your family.

SECTION 3 Life With Carbon

DISCOVER

ACTIVITY

What Is in Milk?

1. Pour 30 mL of milk into a plastic cup.

2. Pour another 30 mL of milk into a second plastic cup. Rinse the graduated cylinder. Measure 15 mL of vinegar and add it to the second cup. Swirl the two liquids together and let the mixture sit for a minute.

3. Set up two funnels with filter paper, each supported in a narrow plastic cup.

4. Filter the milk through the first funnel. Filter the milk and vinegar through the second funnel.

5. What is left in each filter paper? Examine the liquid that passed through each filter paper.

Think It Over

Observing Where did you see evidence of solids? What do you think was the source of these solids?

Have you ever been told to eat all the organic compounds on your plate? Have you heard how eating a variety of polymers and monomers contributes to good health? What? No one has ever said either of those things to you? Well, maybe what you really heard was something about eating all the vegetables on your plate. Or that you need to eat a variety of foods to give you a healthy balance of carbohydrates, proteins, fats, and other nutrients. Organic compounds are the building blocks of all living things. Foods provide organic compounds, which the cells of living things use or change.

GUIDE FOR READING

◆ What are the four main classes of polymers in living things?

◆ How are the polymers in living things different from each other?

Reading Tip Before you read, rewrite each heading as a question. Then read to answer your questions.

Figure 17 This salad bar offers several tasty mixtures of organic compounds that you can eat.

Nutrients From Foods

Nutrients (NOO tree unts) are substances that provide the energy and raw materials the body needs to grow, repair worn parts, and function properly. Most of the nutrients in foods are organic compounds. Many nutrients are large, chainlike molecules called polymers. Each link in the chain is a small molecule called a monomer.

The body can break apart the large molecules in food into small molecules. The process of breaking polymers into monomers, which involves chemical changes, has the familiar name **digestion.**

After food is digested, the body then breaks apart some of the monomers, which releases energy. The body takes other monomers and reassembles them into polymers that match specific body chemistry. **The four classes of polymers found in all living things are carbohydrates, lipids, proteins, and nucleic acids.**

☑ *Checkpoint* How does your body use nutrients?

Carbohydrates

A **carbohydrate** (kahr boh HY drayt) is an energy-rich organic compound made of the elements carbon, hydrogen, and oxygen. The word *carbohydrate* is made of two parts: *carbo-* and *-hydrate. Carbo-* means "carbon" and *-hydrate* means "combined with

Figure 18 Carbohydrates and other polymers in foods are sources of the energy for these cross-country runners. Glucose is a simple carbohydrate.
Interpreting Diagrams What elements make up a glucose molecule?

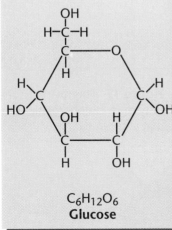

$C_6H_{12}O_6$
Glucose

Figure 19 Grapes and honey contain sugars.

water." If you remember that water is made up of the elements hydrogen and oxygen, then you should be able to remember the three elements in carbohydrates.

Simple Carbohydrates The simplest carbohydrates are sugars. You may be surprised to learn that there are many different kinds of sugars. The sugar listed in baking recipes, which you can buy in bags or boxes at the grocery store, is only one kind. Other sugars are found naturally in fruits, milk, and some vegetables.

One of the most important sugars in your body is **glucose**. Its molecular formula is $C_6H_{12}O_6$. Glucose is sometimes called "blood sugar" because the body circulates glucose to all body parts through the blood. The structural formula for a glucose molecule is shown in Figure 18.

The name of the white sugar that sweetens cookies, candies, and many soft drinks is sucrose. It is a more complex molecule than glucose and has a molecular formula of $C_{12}H_{22}O_{11}$.

Complex Carbohydrates When you eat plants or food products made from plants, you are often eating complex carbohydrates. Each molecule of a simple carbohydrate, or sugar, is relatively small compared to a molecule of a complex carbohydrate. A **complex carbohydrate** is made of a long chain of simple carbohydrates bonded to each other. Just one molecule of a complex carbohydrate may have hundreds of carbon atoms.

Two of the complex carbohydrates assembled from glucose molecules are starch and cellulose. **Starch and cellulose are both built from glucose monomers, but the monomers are arranged differently in each case.** So starch and cellulose are different compounds. They serve different functions in the plants that form them. The body also uses starch from foods very differently from the way it uses cellulose.

Figure 20 Starchy foods (left) provide energy. Foods high in cellulose (right) provide fiber.
Interpreting Photographs Name examples of foods high in starch and foods high in cellulose.

Starch Plants store energy in the form of the complex carbohydrate **starch.** You can find starches in food products made from wheat grains, such as bread, cereal, and pasta. Starches are also found in rice, potatoes, and other vegetables. The body digests the large starch molecules from these foods into individual glucose molecules. Then the body breaks apart the glucose and releases energy.

Cellulose Plants build strong stems and roots with the complex carbohydrate **cellulose** and other polymers. If you imagine yourself crunching on a stick of celery, you will be able to imagine what cellulose is like. Most fruits, vegetables, and nuts are high in cellulose. So are food products made from whole grains. Even though the body can break down starch, the body cannot break down cellulose into individual glucose molecules. Therefore the body cannot use cellulose as a source of energy. In fact, when you eat foods with cellulose, the molecules pass right through you undigested. However, this undigested cellulose helps keep your digestive track active and healthy. Cellulose is sometimes called fiber.

☑ *Checkpoint* *What is cellulose?*

Proteins

If the proteins in your body suddenly disappeared, you would not have much of a body left! Your muscles, hair, skin, and fingernails are all made of proteins. A bird's feathers, a spider's web, a fish's scales, and the horns of a rhinoceros are also made of proteins.

Chains of Amino Acids The polymers called **proteins** are made of organic compounds called amino acids. That means that **amino acids** are the monomers in a protein molecule. **Unlike the sugars in complex carbohydrates, the monomers in a protein are not exactly alike. In fact, there are 20 different kinds of amino acids!**

Amino acids are made of the elements carbon, nitrogen, oxygen, and hydrogen, and sometimes sulfur. The structure of valine, one of the amino acids, is shown in Figure 21. Each amino acid molecule has a carboxyl group (-COOH), like other organic acids. The *acid* part of the term *amino acid* comes from "organic acid." An amine group (-NH$_2$) is the source of the *amino* half of the name.

A huge variety of proteins are made by living things. Each protein molecule may contain a combination of hundreds of amino acids. With 20 kinds of amino acids, millions of amino acid combinations are possible.

Food Proteins Become Your Proteins Some of the best sources of protein include meat, fish, eggs, and milk or milk products. Some plant products such as beans are good sources of protein as well. If you did the Discover activity, you used vinegar to separate proteins from milk.

The body uses proteins from food to build and repair body parts. But the body must first break apart the protein polymers into monomers. Remember that starch is digested into individual glucose molecules. In the same way, proteins are digested into individual amino acids. Then the body reassembles those amino acids into thousands of proteins.

Valine

Figure 21 These foods are all good sources of protein. Protein polymers are built from long chains of amino acids. Valine is one example of an amino acid.

Figure 22 The labels on some bottles of cooking oil tell you that they are low in saturated fats or high in polyunsaturated oils. These foods (right) are high in animal fats or vegetable oils. *Classifying Which class of organic compounds includes the fats and oils?*

Figure 23 Cholesterol deposits in this artery (shown in cross section) have narrowed the space available for blood to flow through.

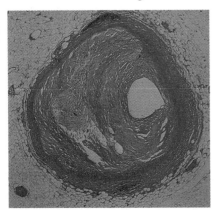

Lipids

The third class of organic compounds in living things is lipids. Like carbohydrates, **lipids** are energy-rich polymers made of carbon, oxygen, and hydrogen. Lipids include fats, oils, waxes, and cholesterol. **Gram for gram, lipids store more than twice as much energy as do carbohydrates.** Lipids behave somewhat like hydrocarbons—the compounds of carbon and hydrogen you read about in Section 2. They mix poorly with water.

Fats and Oils Have you ever gotten grease on your clothes from foods that contain fats or oils? Fats are found in foods such as meat, butter, and cheese. Oils in foods include those such as corn oil, sunflower oil, peanut oil, and olive oil.

Fats and oils have the same basic structure. Each fat or oil polymer is made of three **fatty acid** monomers and one alcohol monomer named glycerol, as shown in *Exploring the Polymers of Life.* There is one main difference between fats and oils, however. Fats are usually solid at room temperature, whereas oils are liquid. You have to heat butter, for example, to make it melt. The temperature at which a fat or oil becomes a liquid depends on the chemical structure of its fatty acid molecules.

You may hear fats and oils described as "saturated" or "unsaturated." Like saturated hydrocarbons, the fatty acids of saturated fats have no double bonds between carbon atoms. Unsaturated fatty acids are found in oils. Monounsaturated oils have fatty acids with one double bond. Polyunsaturated oils have fatty acids with many double bonds. (Remember that *mono* means "one" and *poly* means "many.") Saturated fats tend to have higher melting points than unsaturated oils do.

Cholesterol Another important lipid is **cholesterol** (kuh LES tuh rawl), a waxy substance found in all animal cells. The body builds cell structures from cholesterol and uses it to form compounds that serve as chemical messengers. The body produces the cholesterol it needs from

INTEGRATING
HEALTH

other nutrients. But foods that come from animals—cheese, eggs, and meat—also provide cholesterol. Foods from plant sources, such as vegetable oils, never contain cholesterol.

Although saturated fats are often found in the same foods as cholesterol, they are different compounds. Excess levels of cholesterol in the blood can contribute to heart disease. But saturated fats can affect the levels of cholesterol in the blood. For this reason it is wise to limit your intake of both nutrients.

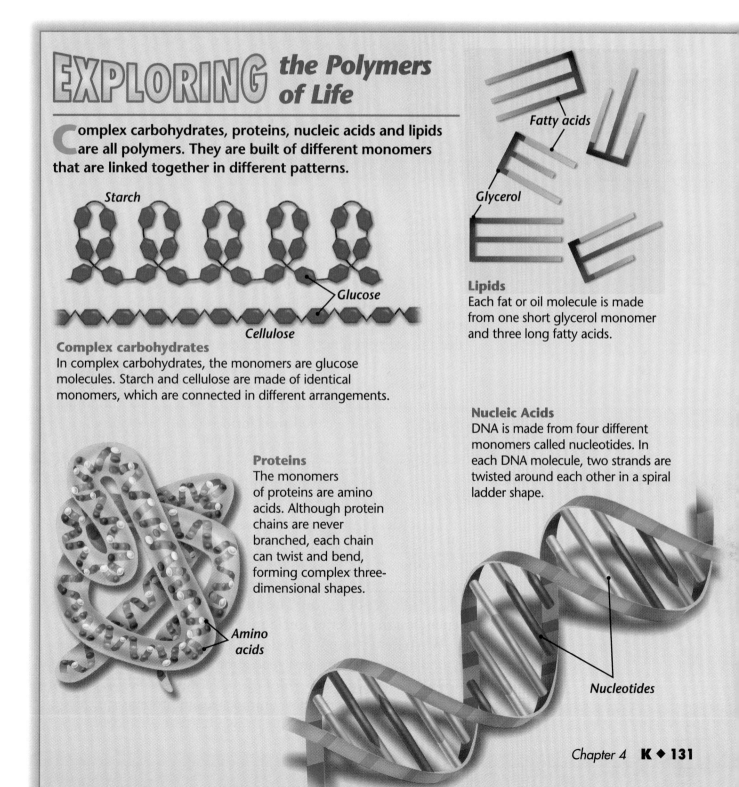

EXPLORING the Polymers of Life

Complex carbohydrates, proteins, nucleic acids and lipids are all polymers. They are built of different monomers that are linked together in different patterns.

Starch

Glucose

Cellulose

Complex carbohydrates
In complex carbohydrates, the monomers are glucose molecules. Starch and cellulose are made of identical monomers, which are connected in different arrangements.

Proteins
The monomers of proteins are amino acids. Although protein chains are never branched, each chain can twist and bend, forming complex three-dimensional shapes.

Amino acids

Fatty acids

Glycerol

Lipids
Each fat or oil molecule is made from one short glycerol monomer and three long fatty acids.

Nucleic Acids
DNA is made from four different monomers called nucleotides. In each DNA molecule, two strands are twisted around each other in a spiral ladder shape.

Nucleotides

Figure 24 This hummingbird and the flower it is visiting (left) are different living things because their DNA differs. Scientists who study DNA in humans and other living things compare the patterns of bands in test data called DNA fingerprints (right).

Nucleic Acids

The fourth class of organic polymers in living things is made up of nucleic acids. **Nucleic acids** (noo KLEE ik) are very large organic compounds made up of carbon, oxygen, hydrogen, nitrogen, and phosphorus. You have probably heard of **DNA,** the initials that stand for one type of nucleic acid, called deoxyribonucleic acid (dee ahk see ry boh noo KLEE ik). The other type of nucleic acid, ribonucleic acid (ry boh noo KLEE ic), is called **RNA.**

Like other polymers, DNA and RNA are made of different kinds of small molecules connected in a pattern. The monomers of nucleic acids are called **nucleotides** (NOO klee oh tydz). In even the simplest living things, the DNA contains billions of nucleotides! There are only four kinds of nucleotides in DNA. RNA is also built of only four kinds of nucleotides, similar to the DNA monomers.

The order of the nucleotides serves as coded instructions to cells, the basic structure of living things. The DNA of one living thing differs from the DNA of other living things. Therefore, the cells in a hummingbird grow and function differently from the cells in a flower or in you. **The differences among living things depend on the order of nucleotides in the DNA.**

When living things reproduce, they pass DNA and the information it carries to the next generation. The order of nucleotides in DNA determines the order of nucleotides in RNA. That in turn determines the order of amino acids in proteins.

Other Nutrients in Foods

The four classes of polymers are not the only compounds your body needs. Your body also needs vitamins and minerals. Unlike the nutrients discussed so far, vitamins and minerals are needed in only small amounts. They do not directly provide you with energy or raw materials.

Vitamins are organic compounds that serve as helper molecules in a variety of chemical reactions in your body. For example, vitamin C, or ascorbic acid, is important for keeping your skin and gums healthy. Vitamin D helps develop your bones and teeth and keep them strong.

Minerals are elements needed by your body. Unlike the other nutrients discussed in this chapter, minerals are not organic compounds. You may remember the names of some of the minerals from the periodic table—for example, the elements sodium, calcium, iron, iodine, and potassium.

If you eat a variety of foods, you will probably get the vitamins and minerals you need. Food manufacturers add some vitamins and minerals to packaged foods to replace vitamins and minerals lost in food processing. Such foods say "enriched" on their labels. Sometimes manufacturers add extra vitamins and minerals to foods to "fortify," or strengthen, the nutrient qualities of the food. For example, milk is usually fortified with vitamins A and D.

Figure 25 Vitamins and minerals occur naturally in foods, but food manufacturers also sometimes add vitamins and minerals.
Interpreting Photos What do the packages of these food products tell you about the addition of vitamins and minerals ?

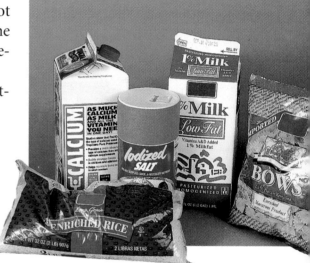

Section 3 Review

1. List an example of each of the four classes of polymers that living things make and use.
2. Compare the monomers of complex carbohydrates and the monomers of proteins.
3. How do lipids and carbohydrates compare as energy-rich polymers?
4. How does the DNA differ for different living things?
5. What nutrients do you need besides the main classes of polymers?
6. **Thinking Critically Making Judgments** Would it matter if you ate foods that provide only carbohydrates but not proteins? Explain your answer.

Check Your Progress
Review the compounds mentioned in this section, and try to find as many as you can on each food label you collected. Prepare a table that will organize your data. Be sure to include entries for carbohydrates (including sugars), proteins, and lipids (including fats, oils, and cholesterol.) Also include entries for vitamins and minerals (for example, the element sodium). You may also want to keep track of ingredients you cannot identify. (*Hint:* Manufacturers may add compounds to improve the flavor or texture of a food, prevent it from spoiling, or give it a longer shelf-life.)

CHAPTER PROJECT 4

Are You Getting Your Vitamins?

Many fruit juices naturally contain vitamin C. Manufacturers add vitamin C to some fruit-flavored drinks and sports drinks. In this lab, you will find out what has the most vitamin C: orange juice, apple juice, a fruit-flavored drink, or a sports drink.

Problem

How much vitamin C is found in different beverages?

Skills Focus

measuring, predicting, designing experiments, drawing conclusions

Materials

6 small paper cups
6 plastic droppers
starch solution
iodine solution
vitamin C solution
samples of beverages to be tested (orange juice, apple juice, sports drink, fruit-flavored drink)

Procedure

Part 1 Vitamin C Test

1. Using a plastic dropper, place 25 drops of tap water into one of the small cups. Add 2 drops of starch solution.

2. Add 1 drop of iodine solution to the cup. **CAUTION:** *Iodine solution can stain skin or clothing.* Observe the color of the mixture. Save this cup to use for comparison in Step 4.

3. Using a fresh dropper, place 25 drops of vitamin C solution into another cup. Add 2 drops of starch solution.

4. Add 1 drop of iodine solution to the cup and swirl. Continue adding iodine a drop at a time, swirling after each drop, until you get a dark blue color similar to the color obtained in Step 2. Record the number of iodine drops.

5. Save the cup from Step 4 and use it for comparison during Part 2.

Part 2 Comparison Test

6. Which beverage sample do you think has the most vitamin C? Which do you think has the least? Rank your beverage samples according to your predictions.

7. Adapt the procedure from Part 1 so you can compare the amount of vitamin C in your beverage samples to the vitamin C solution.

8. Make a data table in your notebook similar to the one on the next page.

9. Carry out your procedure after your teacher approves.

DATA TABLE

Test Sample	Drops of Iodine	Predicted Rank	Actual Rank
vitamin C			
orange juice			
apple juice			
sport drink			
fruit-flavored drink			

Analyze and Conclude

1. What was the purpose for the test of the mixture of starch and water in Step 2?

2. What was the purpose for the test of the starch, water, and vitamin C in Step 4?

3. What do you think caused differences between your data from Step 2 and Step 4?

4. Why did you have to add the same amount of starch to each of the beverages?

5. What would happen if someone forgot to add the starch to the beverage before they began adding iodine?

6. Of the four drinks you tested, which took the most drops of iodine before changing color? Which took the fewest?

7. Which beverage had the most vitamin C? Which had the least? How do you know?

8. When you tested orange juice, the color of the first few drops of the iodine faded away. What do you think happened to the iodine?

9. **Apply** If a beverage scored low in your test for vitamin C, does that mean it isn't good for you? What other factors might make a beverage nutritious or take away from its nutrient value?

Design an Experiment

Foods are often labeled with expiration dates. Labels often also say to "refrigerate after opening." Design an experiment to find out if the vitamin C content of orange juice changes over time at different temperatures. Check your plans with your teacher before you try the experiment.

Natural or Artificial—A Sweet Dilemma

Do you have a sweet tooth? Many people do. But there is a price to be paid for sweetness. Excess energy from sugars is easily stored by the body in the form of fat. The bacteria that cause tooth decay use sugars in the mouth as food. And for people who have the disease diabetes, sugary foods can raise blood sugar to a life-threatening level.

Food scientists have developed three organic compounds that taste sweet but provide few calories—saccharin, cyclamate, and aspartame. Aspartame, for example, is 200 times as sweet as the sugar sucrose. Gram for gram, aspartame and sucrose have equal calories. But it takes much smaller amounts of aspartame to give the same sweetness. Unfortunately, saccharin, cyclamate, and aspartame all have health risks associated with their use.

The Issues

Why Use Artificial Sweeteners? Artificial sweeteners allow people with diabetes to enjoy sweet foods and beverages safely without raising their blood sugar level. But most people who consume artificial sweeteners want to lose weight. Advertising has glamorized being thin. In addition, being overweight can lead to serious health conditions, such as heart disease and high blood pressure.

What Are Possible Dangers? Studies of cyclamate have shown that large doses can lead to cancer and birth defects in lab animals. The U.S. Food and Drug Administration (FDA) has banned cyclamate, but some people think that cyclamate would be safe in moderate amounts.

In similar studies of saccharin, large doses seem to cause cancer in lab animals. Long-term studies with people have not provided clear results. Some people think any risk is too much. The FDA, therefore, requires all products containing saccharin to have labels warning of possible health risks.

Early tests on aspartame showed it to be safe. But long-term studies suggest some problems with heavy use. More testing is needed. For about one in every ten thousand people, the use of aspartame can be very dangerous. If a person has the genetic disorder called phenylketonuria (PKU), then one of the amino acids in aspartame can interfere with normal development. These people must avoid aspartame, especially as infants.

How Much Is Too Much? Different people have different health concerns. Thus the question of how much sugar or artificial sweetener is too much depends on the individual. For some people, no artificial sweeteners is the answer. For others, moderate amounts, such as one or two servings a day, may be safe. But more scientific evidence must be collected to answer how much is too much.

You Decide

1. Identify the Problem
In your own words, explain the issues about the use of artificial sweeteners.

2. Analyze the Options
List the pros and cons for using artificial sweeteners as well as the pros and cons for using sugar.

3. Find a Solution
You are planning refreshments for a school event. Should you provide artificially sweetened soft drinks? Write a brief statement supporting your opinion.

SECTION 1 — Chemical Bonds, Carbon Style

Key Ideas

◆ Carbon can form a large number of different compounds because each carbon atom can form four bonds.

◆ The element carbon exists in different forms. Diamond crystals are the hardest mineral formed in Earth. Graphite is a slippery form of carbon. Fullerenes, or bucky balls, were first made in 1985.

Key Terms
diamond
graphite
fullerene

SECTION 2 — Carbon Compounds

Key Ideas

◆ Many organic compounds have properties in common with each other.

◆ Carbon chains in hydrocarbons can be straight, branched, or ring-shaped.

◆ Isomers are different from each other due to their differing structural formula.

◆ Substituted hydrocarbons, which are related to other hydrocarbons, include halogen compounds, alcohols, and organic acids.

◆ Polymers are formed from many monomers linked together.

Key Terms
organic compound   hydroxyl group
hydrocarbon   alcohol
molecular formula   organic acid
subscript   carboxyl group
structural formula   ester
isomer   polymer
saturated hydrocarbon   monomer
unsaturated hydrocarbon   synthetic
substituted hydrocarbon

SECTION 3 — Life With Carbon

INTEGRATING LIFE SCIENCE

Key Ideas

◆ Nutrients provide your body with energy and raw materials. Many nutrients are organic compounds with large polymer molecules.

◆ The four main classes of polymers in living things are carbohydrates, proteins, lipids, and nucleic acids.

◆ The monomers of complex carbohydrates are simple sugars. The monomers of proteins are amino acids. The monomers of fats and oils are fatty acids and glycerol. The monomers of nucleic acids are nucleotides.

◆ Vitamins and minerals are other nutrients that contribute to a healthy diet.

Key Terms
nutrient   lipid
digestion   fatty acid
carbohydrate   cholesterol
glucose   nucleic acid
complex carbohydrate   DNA
starch   RNA
cellulose   nucleotide
protein   vitamin
amino acid   mineral

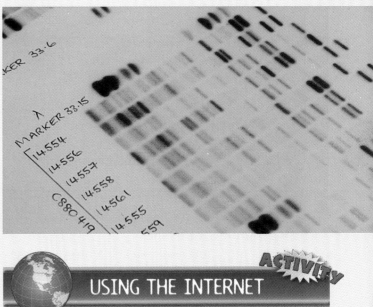

USING THE INTERNET

ACTIVITY

www.science-explorer.phschool.com

Reviewing Content

For more review of key concepts, see the Interactive Student Tutorial CD-ROM.

Multiple Choice

Choose the letter of the best answer.

1. The number of valence electrons for each carbon atom is
   a. one.
   b. two.
   c. three.
   d. four.
2. All organic compounds contain
   a. oxygen.
   b. carbon.
   c. halogens.
   d. carboxyl groups.
3. The group —COOH is characteristic of
   a. an organic acid.
   b. an alcohol.
   c. a halogen compound.
   d. a hydrocarbon.
4. The monomers in complex carbohydrates are
   a. sugars.
   b. amino acids.
   c. nucleotides.
   d. fats.
5. Cholesterol is a type of
   a. nucleic acid.
   b. carbohydrate.
   c. lipid.
   d. cellulose.

True or False

If the statement is true, write true. If it is false, change the underlined word or words to make the statement true.

6. Because the bonds between layers of carbon atoms are weak, layers of <u>fullerenes</u> slide easily past one another.
7. Hydrocarbons that contain only single bonds are said to be <u>unsaturated</u>.
8. An <u>organic acid</u> is characterized by one or more atoms of fluorine, chlorine, bromine, or iodine.
9. A <u>monomer</u> is a long chain of <u>polymers</u>.
10. Proteins are made up of long chains of <u>amino acids</u>.

Checking Concepts

11. What is a chemical bond?
12. What do diamonds, graphite, and fullerenes have in common?
13. How would you notice the presence of esters in a fruit such as a pineapple or banana?
14. Starches and cellulose are both complex carbohydrates. How does your body handle these compounds differently?
15. Compare and contrast the fatty acids in fats that are solid at room temperature with fatty acids in oils that are liquids.
16. Why is the order of nucleotides in DNA important?
17. **Writing to Learn** Write at least ten riddles for different forms of carbon and for organic compounds. Riddles are problems or puzzles usually worded as a question. For example, "What is made of carbon atoms and is shaped like a soccer ball?" Try to be original. Write each riddle on the front of an index card and the correct answer on the back. Then share your riddles with your classmates and see if they can solve them.

Thinking Visually

18. **Venn Diagram** Copy the Venn diagram about proteins and nucleic acids onto a separate sheet of paper. Then complete it and add a title. (See the Skills Handbook for more on Venn diagrams.)

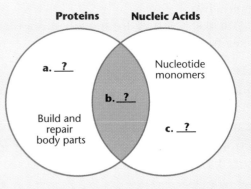

Applying Skills

Use the following structural formulas to answer Questions 19–22.

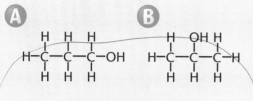

A   **B**

19. **Classifying** Which type of substituted hydrocarbons are compounds A and B? What information in the structural formulas did you use to decide your answer?

20. **Observing** What is the correct subscript for the carbon atoms (C) in the molecular formula that corresponds to each structural formula?

21. **Inferring** Are compounds A and B isomers? How can you tell?

22. **Predicting** Would you expect these two compounds to have identical properties or different properties? Explain why.

Thinking Critically

23. **Relating Cause and Effect** What features of the element carbon allow it to form the "backbone" of such a varied array of different compounds?

24. **Applying Concepts** CH_4 is a one-carbon saturated hydrocarbon. Why must unsaturated hydrocarbons have a minimum of two carbons?

25. **Classifying** Classify each of the following compounds as a hydrocarbon, an alcohol, an organic acid, or a halogen compound: $C_{12}H_{20}COOH$, C_7H_{16}, C_2H_5Cl, C_4H_7OH.

26. **Posing Questions** Glucose and fructose are both simple carbohydrates with the formula $C_6H_{12}O_6$. What else do you need to know about glucose and fructose to decide if they should be considered different compounds?

27. **Comparing and Contrasting** How are vitamins similar to nutrients such as lipids, carbohydrates, and proteins? How are they different?

Performance Assessment

CHAPTER PROJECT 4 — Wrap Up

Present Your Project Display your data table classifying compounds in foods, along with the labels from which you collected your data. Point out the nutrients that are found in almost all foods and the nutrients found in only a few foods.

Reflect and Record In your journal, list any questions that you were unable to answer in your research. What would you like to learn more about? How could you learn more about substances used in various food products?

Getting Involved

In Your School Create a poster to teach other students in your school about hydrocarbons. Which compounds might they encounter and where? Decide how to represent examples of hydrocarbons visually. Use captions and labels to clearly explain the differences between saturated and unsaturated hydrocarbons. Also compare and contrast different types of substituted hydrocarbons. Display your poster in the school library or in a school corridor.

SOAP
The Dirt Chaser

What slippery substance . . .

- makes things cleaner, fresher, brighter?
- can you put on your head and on your floors?
- greases parts of equipment that might stick?
- rids your hands of germs?

It's soap, which is a cleaner made from materials that are found in nature. People figured out how to make soap by heating natural fats or oils, alkali (a chemical they got from wood ashes), and water. Detergent is also a cleaner. It's similar to soap, but made from manufactured materials.

The average American uses about 11 kilograms of soap per year just to keep clean! Some of that soap is used for baths and showers. Soap is also used by medical experts to clean wounds and prevent infection.

In your home you use soaps and detergents to clean dishes, laundry, windows, floors, and much more. Even factories use soaps in the process of making products such as rubber, jewelry, aluminum, antifreeze, leather, and glossy paper.

So, if you lived without soap, you and your surroundings would be a lot dirtier! You would look and feel quite different. You may just owe your way of life to soap!

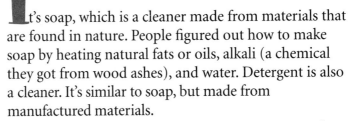

Soapsuds are at work in a baby's bath (top), when washing a dog (middle), and at a car wash (bottom).

Soap Molecule

Mixes well with water

Mixes well with grease and dirt

How Soap Works

You rub shampoo and water into your hair.

Soap molecules in shampoo loosen the grease and dirt on your hair.

Soap molecules break the dirt into tiny pieces.

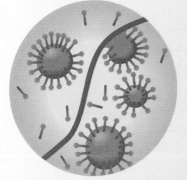

Water carries away the dirt surrounded by soap molecules.

Wash the Dirt Away

Soap manufacturers claim that their products can wash away the dirt from the dirtiest clothes. How does that work? First, you need to wet the clothes with water that contains soap. The soap then spreads out and soaks into the material.

Each molecule of soap is shaped like a tiny tadpole. The tail-like end is similar to a hydrocarbon molecule. It mixes poorly with water, but it mixes well with dirt and grease. The large end, on the other hand, mixes well with water. When you wash, the soap molecules surround the dirt and break it up into tiny pieces that water can wash away.

Some dirt is difficult to dissolve. It takes longer for the soap molecules to loosen it. In these cases rubbing, scrubbing, and squeezing may help to lift the dirt.

Some water, called hard water, has minerals dissolved in it—calcium, magnesium, and iron. In hard water, soap forms deposits, called scum. Scum doesn't dissolve and is difficult to wash away. It keeps clean hair from being shiny and leaves a "bathtub ring."

The invention of detergents helped solve the problem of scum and stubborn stains. For many cleaning tasks, detergent is more effective than soap. Detergent also dissolves in cold water more easily than soap.

The Development of Soap

People have made soap for at least 2,300 years. The ancient Babylonians, Arabs, Greeks, Romans, and Celts made and sometimes traded it. The English word comes from "saipo," the Celts' name for soap. But these early cultures used soap primarily as a hair dye or a medicine, not as a cleaner! Only in the period from A.D. 100–199 did soap become known as a cleaning agent.

Soapmaking in Western Europe began about A.D. 100. First France was a leading producer, then Italy by 700, and Spain by 800. England didn't begin making soap until about 1200. But even then, most people didn't use soap for bathing.

Around 1790, Nicolas Leblanc, a French scientist, discovered that alkali could be made from common table salt and water. After that, soap could be made more easily and sold for profit.

In North America beginning around 1650, colonists made their own soap. Families would make up to a year's supply for their own use. Then around 1800, some people started collecting waste fats and ashes from their neighbors and making soap in large quantities. Soon bars of soap were sold from door to door.

In 1806, William Colgate, a soap and candle maker, started a business called Colgate and Company. His company produced soap and another cleaner, toothpaste. Today, nearly all soap is made in factories using large machinery.

In the boiling room of a French soapmaking factory in the 1870s, workers stir and ladle hot soap.

The first detergent was produced in Germany around 1916, during World War I. Because fats were in short supply, detergent was meant to be a substitute for fat-based soap. However, people found that detergent was a better cleaner than soap for many purposes. The first household detergents appeared in the United States in 1933.

Social Studies Activity

Create a time line of important events in the history of soapmaking. Find photos or make illustrations for the time line. Include the following events:

- early uses and users of soap
- beginning of the soapmaking industry
- early North American soapmaking
- first detergent

Before they discovered soap, what do you think people in earlier times used as a cleaner?

Colonial Soapmaking

Making soap in North America in the 1600s was an exhausting, unpleasant process. For months, colonists saved barrels of ashes from their wood fires. Then they poured hot water over the ashes. An alkali solution, called lye, dripped out of a spigot in the bottom of the barrel.

In a large kettle over a roaring outdoor fire, they boiled the alkali solution with fat, such as greases, which they had also saved. They had to keep the fire high and hot and stir the mixture for hours. When it was thick, they ladled the liquid soap into shallow boxes. Families made soap in the spring and sometimes again in the fall.

The following passage is from the novel *The Iron Peacock* by Mary Stetson Clarke. The story takes place in 1650 in Massachusetts Bay Colony. In the passage, two large supports hold a crossbar where the pot is hung over the fire. The women stir the pot with a homemade tool.

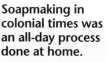

Soapmaking in colonial times was an all-day process done at home.

The next morning was fair, the air washed sparkling clear. Duncan built a fire under the framework. Maura measured the grease, adding a quantity of lye. Ross and Duncan placed the crossbar under the handle of the pot and raised it until it rested on the supports. Maura took up a long wooden bar with a shorter one set at right angles to it, and began stirring the contents of the pot.

"We'll be back at noon to lend you a hand," said Duncan.

Maura and Joanna took turns stirring the soap. When Maura judged it to be of the right consistency, they let the fire die down.

After the men had lifted the pot off the fire, Joanna and Maura ladled the thick brown liquid into boxes lined with old pieces of cloth.

It cooled quickly into thick cream-colored slabs. Maura would cut it into cakes in a few days, when it was solid enough to handle. Then she would stack the bars in a dry place where the air could circulate around them until the soap had seasoned enough for use.

Language Arts Activity

Reread the passage and list the steps for making soap. Think of a process or activity that you know well. It can be packing for a trip or preparing for a party. Jot down the steps and number them. Then, write a description of the process. Include steps and details so that a reader unfamiliar with your activity would know how to do it.

Chemistry of Soap

How is soap made? It's the product of heating two types of compounds—an acid and a base. Acids and bases are compounds that have physical and chemical properties opposite to each other. An acid tastes sour. Grapefruits, pickles, and vinegar have acids in them. A base has properties that make it taste bitter and feel slippery. Bases and acids combine to neutralize each other.

Natural fats and oils are the source of the acids in soapmaking. Fats and oils are polymers, made of three fatty acid monomers and an alcohol called glycerol. In soapmaking, the fatty acids combine with an alkali solution (made of bases). The mixture is processed using water and heat. The resulting chemical reaction is called saponification. Saponification produces the main material of soaps, called "neat" soap. The glycerol left over, also called glycerin, is pumped away.

The difference between solid and liquid soaps depends on the alkali that's added. In a solid soap, the alkali solution is the base sodium hydroxide. In liquid soaps, the alkali solution is the base potassium hydroxide.

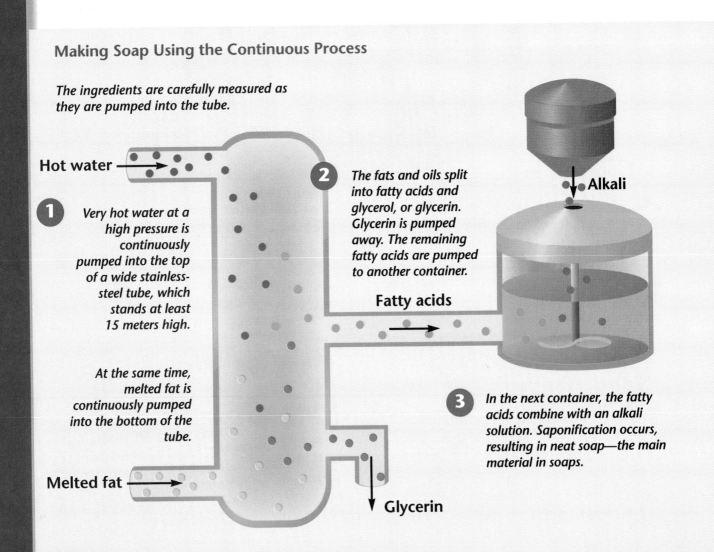

Making Soap Using the Continuous Process

The ingredients are carefully measured as they are pumped into the tube.

Hot water

1 *Very hot water at a high pressure is continuously pumped into the top of a wide stainless-steel tube, which stands at least 15 meters high.*

At the same time, melted fat is continuously pumped into the bottom of the tube.

Melted fat

2 *The fats and oils split into fatty acids and glycerol, or glycerin. Glycerin is pumped away. The remaining fatty acids are pumped to another container.*

Fatty acids

Alkali

3 *In the next container, the fatty acids combine with an alkali solution. Saponification occurs, resulting in neat soap—the main material in soaps.*

Glycerin

Soapmaking

After saponification occurs, neat soap is poured into molds. Other ingredients are sometimes added at this stage. Then the bars are stamped with a brand name or designed and wrapped for shipment.

To make cosmetic soaps, an additional process called milling is needed. The neat soap is poured into large slabs instead of into molds. When the slab cools, several sets of rollers press and crush it. This process makes finer, gentler soaps that people can use on their face and hands.

At this stage, a variety of other ingredients can be added, such as scents, colors, or germicides (to kill bacteria). Air can be whipped into soap to make it float. Soapmakers compete to find the combination of ingredients that will be most attractive and smell pleasant to customers.

4 Neat soap is poured into molds and allowed to harden. Before neat soap is made into bars, flakes, or powdered soap, other optional ingredients such as abrasives (scrubbing agents) can be added.

5 Cosmetic soaps require an additional process. After the neat soap cools, it goes through the milling process. The soap is fed through rollers that crush it. Perfumes and other ingredients can be added at this stage.

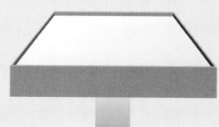

6 The finished soap is pressed, cut, stamped, and wrapped for shipment.

Mathematics

A Year of Soap

What would you do if you had to make a year's supply of your own soap, using modern ingredients? You probably buy the soap you use from a store. But it is still possible to make soap yourself by using the right ingredients and following specific instructions.

Soap recipes are as varied and numerous as food recipes. You can make soap using the oil from avocados, hazelnuts, or sunflower seeds. To add natural scents, you might include rose, cinnamon, cloves, lavender, lemon, mint, grapefruit, pine, rose, vanilla, or something else.

Colors might come from beetroot, cocoa, goldenrod, licorice, paprika, or even seaweed. You can even include "scrubbers" such as cornmeal, oatmeal, or poppy seeds!

Here is the ingredient list for one kind of soap. This recipe makes one bar of soap with a mass of 141.75 grams.

RECIPE FOR SOAP ∽

16.8 grams alkali

45.4 grams water

42.2 grams olive oil

36.2 grams coconut oil

42.2 grams palm oil

❀

Math Activity

Use the list of ingredients to find the answers to these questions:

◆ What is the ratio of alkali to oil in this recipe? Round to the nearest hundredth.

◆ If you made a large batch with a total mass of 1.701 kg, how many bars of soap would you get in that batch?

◆ How much of each ingredient would you need to make this batch?

◆ If your family used two bars of soap per month, how many batches of soap would you make to provide one year's supply?

◆ How many batches would you make if your family used four bars of soap per month through the summer (June, July, and August), two bars per month through the winter (December, January, and February), and three bars per month during the rest of the year?

Tie It Together

Soap Study

Organize a class project to survey and test soaps and soap products that are on the market today. Work in small groups. Choose one kind of cleaner to study, such as bar soaps, dishwashing detergents, laundry detergents, or another cleaner.

As your group investigates one kind of product, answer these questions:

◆ Look at the labels. What kinds of oils and other ingredients are listed?

◆ What do the makers claim these ingredients do? What language do they use to make these claims?

◆ How many kinds of surfaces can you clean with this product?

Next, collect several brands. Design an experiment to help you decide which brand works best.

◆ Decide what you will test for, such as how well the brand cleans grease.

◆ Develop a grading scale for rating the products.

◆ Before you begin, predict what your results will be.

◆ Keep all variables the same except for the brand.

◆ Perform the tests, collect data, and take careful notes.

Decide how to present your results to the class. You might include photographs of the test results, create a graph, or write a report describing and summarizing the results.

Think Like a Scientist

Although you may not know it, you think like a scientist every day. Whenever you ask a question and explore possible answers, you use many of the same skills that scientists do. Some of these skills are described on this page.

Observing

When you use one or more of your five senses to gather information about the world, you are **observing.** Hearing a dog bark, counting twelve green seeds, and smelling smoke are all observations. To increase the power of their senses, scientists sometimes use microscopes, telescopes, or other instruments that help them make more detailed observations.

An observation must be factual and accurate—an exact report of what your senses detect. It is important to keep careful records of your observations in science class by writing or drawing in a notebook. The information collected through observations is called evidence, or data.

Inferring

When you explain or interpret an observation, you are **inferring,** or making an inference. For example, if you hear your dog barking, you may infer that someone is at your front door. To make this inference, you combine the evidence—the barking dog—and your experience or knowledge—you know that your dog barks when strangers approach—to reach a logical conclusion.

Notice that an inference is not a fact; it is only one of many possible explanations for an observation. For example, your dog may be barking because it wants to go for a walk. An inference may turn out to be incorrect even if it is based on accurate observations and logical reasoning. The only way to find out if an inference is correct is to investigate further.

Predicting

When you listen to the weather forecast, you hear many predictions about the next day's weather—what the temperature will be, whether it will rain, and how windy it will be. Weather forecasters use observations and knowledge of weather patterns to predict the weather. The skill of **predicting** involves making an inference about a future event based on current evidence or past experience.

Because a prediction is an inference, it may prove to be false. In science class, you can test some of your predictions by doing experiments. For example, suppose you predict that larger paper airplanes can fly farther than smaller airplanes. How could you test your prediction?

ACTIVITY Use the photograph to answer the questions below.

Observing Look closely at the photograph. List at least three observations.

Inferring Use your observations to make an inference about what has happened. What experience or knowledge did you use to make the inference?

Predicting Predict what will happen next. On what evidence or experience do you base your prediction?

Classifying

Could you imagine searching for a book in the library if the books were shelved in no particular order? Your trip to the library would be an all-day event! Luckily, librarians group together books on similar topics or by the same author. Grouping together items that are alike in some way is called **classifying.** You can classify items in many ways: by size, by shape, by use, and by other important characteristics.

Like librarians, scientists use the skill of classifying to organize information and objects. When things are sorted into groups, the relationships among them become easier to understand.

ACTIVITY

Classify the objects in the photograph into two groups based on any characteristic you choose. Then use another characteristic to classify the objects into three groups.

Making Models

ACTIVITY

This student is using a model to demonstrate what causes day and night on Earth. What do the flashlight and the tennis ball in the model represent?

Have you ever drawn a picture to help someone understand what you were saying? Such a drawing is one type of model. A model is a picture, diagram, computer image, or other representation of a complex object or process. **Making models** helps people understand things that they cannot observe directly.

Scientists often use models to represent things that are either very large or very small, such as the planets in the solar system, or the parts of a cell. Such models are physical models—drawings or three-dimensional structures that look like the real thing. Other models are mental models—mathematical equations or words that describe how something works.

Communicating

Whenever you talk on the phone, write a letter, or listen to your teacher at school, you are communicating. **Communicating** is the process of sharing ideas and information with other people. Communicating effectively requires many skills, including writing, reading, speaking, listening, and making models.

Scientists communicate to share results, information, and opinions. Scientists often communicate about their work in journals, over the telephone, in

letters, and on the Internet. They also attend scientific meetings where they share their ideas with one another in person.

ACTIVITY

On a sheet of paper, write out clear, detailed directions for tying your shoe. Then exchange directions with a partner. Follow your partner's directions exactly. How successful were you at tying your shoe? How could your partner have communicated more clearly?

Making Measurements

When scientists make observations, it is not sufficient to say that something is "big" or "heavy." Instead, scientists use instruments to measure just how big or heavy an object is. By measuring, scientists can express their observations more precisely and communicate more information about what they observe.

Measuring in SI

The standard system of measurement used by scientists around the world is known as the International System of Units, which is abbreviated as SI (in French, *Système International d'Unités*). SI units are easy to use because they are based on multiples of 10. Each unit is ten times larger than the next smallest unit and one tenth the size of the next largest unit. The table lists the prefixes used to name the most common SI units.

Common SI Prefixes		
Prefix	**Symbol**	**Meaning**
kilo-	k	1,000
hecto-	h	100
deka-	da	10
deci-	d	0.1 (one tenth)
centi-	c	0.01 (one hundredth)
milli-	m	0.001 (one thousandth)

Length To measure length, or the distance between two points, the unit of measure is the **meter (m).** One meter is the approximate distance from the floor to a doorknob. Long distances, such as the distance between two cities, are measured in kilometers (km). Small lengths are measured in centimeters (cm) or millimeters (mm). Scientists use metric rulers and meter sticks to measure length.

Common Conversions
1 km = 1,000 m
1 m = 100 cm
1 m = 1,000 mm
1 cm = 10 mm

The larger lines on the metric ruler in the picture show centimeter divisions, while the smaller, unnumbered lines show millimeter divisions. How many centimeters long is the shell? How many millimeters long is it?

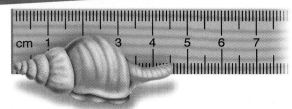

Liquid Volume To measure the volume of a liquid, or the amount of space it takes up, you will use a unit of measure known as the **liter (L).** One liter is the approximate volume of a medium-sized carton of milk. Smaller volumes are measured in milliliters (mL). Scientists use graduated cylinders to measure liquid volume.

Common Conversion
1 L = 1,000 mL

The graduated cylinder in the picture is marked in milliliter divisions. Notice that the water in the cylinder has a curved surface. This curved surface is called the *meniscus.* To measure the volume, you must read the level at the lowest point of the meniscus. What is the volume of water in this graduated cylinder?

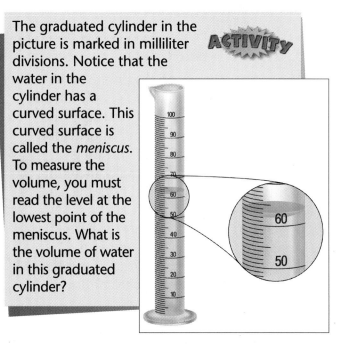

Mass To measure mass, or the amount of matter in an object, you will use a unit of measure known as the **gram (g)**. One gram is approximately the mass of a paper clip. Larger masses are measured in kilograms (kg). Scientists use a balance to find the mass of an object.

Common Conversion
1 kg = 1,000 g

The electronic balance displays the mass of an apple in kilograms. What is the mass of the apple? Suppose a recipe for applesauce called for one kilogram of apples. About how many apples would you need?

ACTIVITY

Temperature
To measure the temperature of a substance, you will use the **Celsius scale**. Temperature is measured in degrees Celsius (°C) using a Celsius thermometer. Water freezes at 0°C and boils at 100°C.

ACTIVITY
What is the temperature of the liquid in degrees Celsius?

Converting SI Units

To use the SI system, you must know how to convert between units. Converting from one unit to another involves the skill of **calculating**, or using mathematical operations. Converting between SI units is similar to converting between dollars and dimes because both systems are based on multiples of ten.

Suppose you want to convert a length of 80 centimeters to meters. Follow these steps to convert between units.

1. Begin by writing down the measurement you want to convert—in this example, 80 centimeters.
2. Write a conversion factor that represents the relationship between the two units you are converting. In this example, the relationship is *1 meter = 100 centimeters*. Write this conversion factor as a fraction, making sure to place the units you are converting from (centimeters, in this example) in the denominator.

3. Multiply the measurement you want to convert by the fraction. When you do this, the units in the first measurement will cancel out with the units in the denominator. Your answer will be in the units you are converting to (meters, in this example).

Example

80 centimeters = ___?___ meters

$$80 \text{ centimeters} \times \frac{1 \text{ meter}}{100 \text{ centimeters}} = \frac{80 \text{ meters}}{100}$$

$$= 0.8 \text{ meters}$$

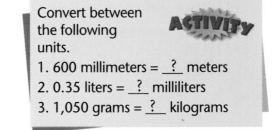

ACTIVITY
Convert between the following units.
1. 600 millimeters = _?_ meters
2. 0.35 liters = _?_ milliliters
3. 1,050 grams = _?_ kilograms

Conducting a Scientific Investigation

In some ways, scientists are like detectives, piecing together clues to learn about a process or event. One way that scientists gather clues is by carrying out experiments. An experiment tests an idea in a careful, orderly manner. Although all experiments do not follow the same steps in the same order, many follow a pattern similar to the one described here.

Posing Questions

Experiments begin by asking a scientific question. A scientific question is one that can be answered by gathering evidence. For example, the question "Which freezes faster—fresh water or salt water?" is a scientific question because you can carry out an investigation and gather information to answer the question.

Developing a Hypothesis

The next step is to form a hypothesis. A **hypothesis** is a prediction about the outcome of the experiment. Like all predictions, hypotheses are based on your observations and previous knowledge or experience. But, unlike many predictions, a hypothesis must be something that can be tested. A properly worded hypothesis should take the form of an *If … then …* statement. For example, a hypothesis might be *"If I add salt to fresh water, then the water will take longer to freeze."* A hypothesis worded this way serves as a rough outline of the experiment you should perform.

Designing an Experiment

Next you need to plan a way to test your hypothesis. Your plan should be written out as a step-by-step procedure and should describe the observations or measurements you will make.

Two important steps involved in designing an experiment are controlling variables and forming operational definitions.

Controlling Variables In a well-designed experiment, you need to keep all variables the same except for one. A **variable** is any factor that can change in an experiment. The factor that you change is called the **manipulated variable.** In this experiment, the manipulated variable is the amount of salt added to the water. Other factors, such as the amount of water or the starting temperature, are kept constant.

The factor that changes as a result of the manipulated variable is called the responding variable. The **responding variable** is what you measure or observe to obtain your results. In this experiment, the responding variable is how long the water takes to freeze.

An experiment in which all factors except one are kept constant is a **controlled experiment.** Most controlled experiments include a test called the control. In this experiment, Container 3 is the control. Because no salt is added to Container 3, you can compare the results from the other containers to it. Any difference in results must be due to the addition of salt alone.

Forming Operational Definitions

Another important aspect of a well-designed experiment is having clear operational definitions. An **operational definition** is a statement that describes how a particular variable is to be measured or how a term is to be defined. For example, in this experiment, how will you determine if the water has frozen? You might decide to insert a stick in each container at the start of the experiment. Your operational definition of "frozen" would be the time at which the stick can no longer move.

EXPERIMENTAL PROCEDURE

1. Fill 3 containers with 300 milliliters of cold tap water.

2. Add 10 grams of salt to Container 1; stir. Add 20 grams of salt to Container 2; stir. Add no salt to Container 3.

3. Place the 3 containers in a freezer.

4. Check the containers every 15 minutes. Record your observations.

Interpreting Data

The observations and measurements you make in an experiment are called data. At the end of an experiment, you need to analyze the data to look for any patterns or trends. Patterns often become clear if you organize your data in a data table or graph. Then think through what the data reveal. Do they support your hypothesis? Do they point out a flaw in your experiment? Do you need to collect more data?

Drawing Conclusions

A conclusion is a statement that sums up what you have learned from an experiment. When you draw a conclusion, you need to decide whether the data you collected support your hypothesis or not. You may need to repeat an experiment several times before you can draw any conclusions from it. Conclusions often lead you to pose new questions and plan new experiments to answer them.

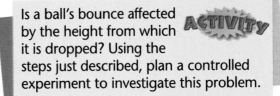

Is a ball's bounce affected by the height from which it is dropped? Using the steps just described, plan a controlled experiment to investigate this problem. **ACTIVITY**

Thinking Critically

Has a friend ever asked for your advice about a problem? If so, you may have helped your friend think through the problem in a logical way. Without knowing it, you used critical-thinking skills to help your friend. Critical thinking involves the use of reasoning and logic to solve problems or make decisions. Some critical-thinking skills are described below.

Comparing and Contrasting

When you examine two objects for similarities and differences, you are using the skill of **comparing and contrasting.** Comparing involves identifying similarities, or common characteristics. Contrasting involves identifying differences. Analyzing objects in this way can help you discover details that you might otherwise overlook.

Compare and contrast the two animals in the photo. First list all the similarities that you see. Then list all the differences.

ACTIVITY

Applying Concepts

When you use your knowledge about one situation to make sense of a similar situation, you are using the skill of **applying concepts.** Being able to transfer your knowledge from one situation to another shows that you truly understand a concept. You may use this skill in answering test questions that present different problems from the ones you've reviewed in class.

You have just learned that water takes longer to freeze when other substances are mixed into it. Use this knowledge to explain why people need a substance called antifreeze in their car's radiator in the winter.

ACTIVITY

Interpreting Illustrations

Diagrams, photographs, and maps are included in textbooks to help clarify what you read. These illustrations show processes, places, and ideas in a visual manner. The skill called **interpreting illustrations** can help you learn from these visual elements. To understand an illustration, take the time to study the illustration along with all the written information that accompanies it. Captions identify the key concepts shown in the illustration. Labels point out the important parts of a diagram or map, while keys identify the symbols used in a map.

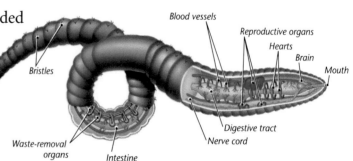

Blood vessels
Reproductive organs
Hearts
Brain
Mouth
Bristles
Digestive tract
Nerve cord
Waste-removal organs
Intestine

▲ **Internal anatomy of an earthworm**

Study the diagram above. Then write a short paragraph explaining what you have learned.

ACTIVITY

Relating Cause and Effect

If one event causes another event to occur, the two events are said to have a cause-and-effect relationship. When you determine that such a relationship exists between two events, you use a skill called **relating cause and effect.** For example, if you notice an itchy, red bump on your skin, you might infer that a mosquito bit you. The mosquito bite is the cause, and the bump is the effect.

It is important to note that two events do not necessarily have a cause-and-effect relationship just because they occur together. Scientists carry out experiments or use past experience to determine whether a cause-and-effect relationship exists.

You are on a camping trip and your flashlight has stopped working. List some possible causes for the flashlight malfunction. How could you determine which cause-and-effect relationship has left you in the dark?

Making Generalizations

When you draw a conclusion about an entire group based on information about only some of the group's members, you are using a skill called **making generalizations.** For a generalization to be valid, the sample you choose must be large enough and representative of the entire group. You might, for example, put this skill to work at a farm stand if you see a sign that says, "Sample some grapes before you buy." If you sample a few sweet grapes, you may conclude that all the grapes are sweet—and purchase a large bunch.

A team of scientists needs to determine whether the water in a large reservoir is safe to drink. How could they use the skill of making generalizations to help them? What should they do?

Making Judgments

When you evaluate something to decide whether it is good or bad, or right or wrong, you are using a skill called **making judgments.** For example, you make judgments when you decide to eat healthful foods or to pick up litter in a park. Before you make a judgment, you need to think through the pros and cons of a situation, and identify the values or standards that you hold.

Should children and teens be required to wear helmets when bicycling? Explain why you feel the way you do.

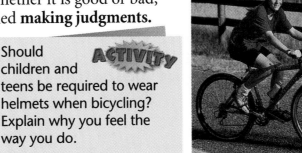

Problem Solving

When you use critical-thinking skills to resolve an issue or decide on a course of action, you are using a skill called **problem solving.** Some problems, such as how to convert a fraction into a decimal, are straightforward. Other problems, such as figuring out why your computer has stopped working, are complex. Some complex problems can be solved using the trial and error method—try out one solution first, and if that doesn't work, try another. Other useful problem-solving strategies include making models and brainstorming possible solutions with a partner.

Organizing Information

As you read this textbook, how can you make sense of all the information it contains? Some useful tools to help you organize information are shown on this page. These tools are called *graphic organizers* because they give you a visual picture of a topic, showing at a glance how key concepts are related.

Concept Maps

Concept maps are useful tools for organizing information on broad topics. A concept map begins with a general concept and shows how it can be broken down into more specific concepts. In that way, relationships between concepts become easier to understand.

A concept map is constructed by placing concept words (usually nouns) in ovals and connecting them with linking words. Often, the most general concept word is placed at the top, and the words become more specific as you move downward. Often the linking words, which are written on a line extending between two ovals, describe the relationship between the two concepts they connect. If you follow any string of concepts and linking words down the map, it should read like a sentence.

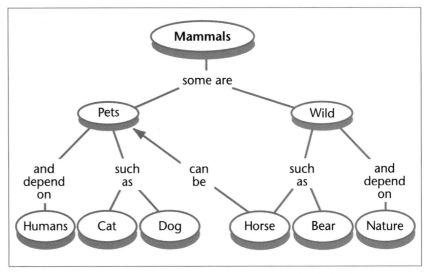

Some concept maps include linking words that connect a concept on one branch of the map to a concept on another branch. These linking words, called cross-linkages, show more complex interrelationships among concepts.

Compare/Contrast Tables

Compare/contrast tables are useful tools for sorting out the similarities and differences between two or more items. A table provides an organized framework in which to compare items based on specific characteristics that you identify.

To create a compare/contrast table, list the items to be compared across the top of a table. Then list the characteristics that will form the basis of your comparison in the left-hand column. Complete the table by filling in information about each characteristic, first for one item and then for the other.

Characteristic	Baseball	Basketball
Number of Players	9	5
Playing Field	Baseball diamond	Basketball court
Equipment	Bat, baseball, mitts	Basket, basketball

Venn Diagrams

Another way to show similarities and differences between items is with a Venn diagram. A Venn diagram consists of two or more circles that partially overlap. Each circle represents a particular concept or idea. Common characteristics, or similarities, are written within the area of overlap between the two circles. Unique characteristics, or differences, are written in the parts of the circles outside the area of overlap.

To create a Venn diagram, draw two overlapping circles. Label the circles with the names of the items being compared. Write the

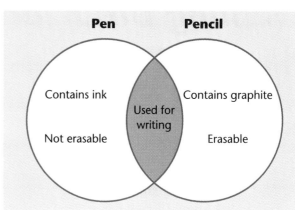

unique characteristics in each circle outside the area of overlap. Then write the shared characteristics within the area of overlap.

Flowcharts

A flowchart can help you understand the order in which certain events have occurred or should occur. Flowcharts are useful for outlining the stages in a process or the steps in a procedure.

To make a flowchart, write a brief description of each event in a box. Place the first event at the top of the page, followed by the second event, the third event, and so on. Then draw an arrow to connect each event to the one that occurs next.

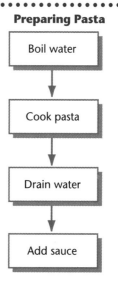

Cycle Diagrams

A cycle diagram can be used to show a sequence of events that is continuous, or cyclical. A continuous sequence does not have an end because, when the final event is over, the first event begins again. Like a flowchart, a cycle diagram can help you understand the order of events.

To create a cycle diagram, write a brief description of each event in a box. Place one event at the top of the page in the center. Then, moving in a clockwise direction around an imaginary circle, write each event in its proper sequence. Draw arrows that connect each event to the one that occurs next, forming a continuous circle.

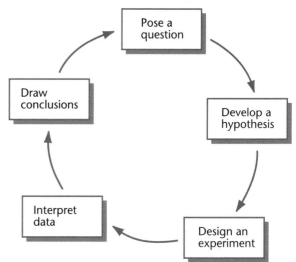

Creating Data Tables and Graphs

How can you make sense of the data in a science experiment? The first step is to organize the data to help you understand them. Data tables and graphs are helpful tools for organizing data.

Data Tables

You have gathered your materials and set up your experiment. But before you start, you need to plan a way to record what happens during the experiment. By creating a data table, you can record your observations and measurements in an orderly way.

Suppose, for example, that a scientist conducted an experiment to find out how many Calories people of different body masses burn while doing various activities. The data table shows the results.

Notice in this data table that the manipulated variable (body mass) is the heading of one column. The responding variable (for Experiment 1, the number of Calories burned while bicycling) is the heading of the next column. Additional columns were added for related experiments.

CALORIES BURNED IN 30 MINUTES OF ACTIVITY

Body Mass	Experiment 1 Bicycling	Experiment 2 Playing Basketball	Experiment 3 Watching Television
30 kg	60 Calories	120 Calories	21 Calories
40 kg	77 Calories	164 Calories	27 Calories
50 kg	95 Calories	206 Calories	33 Calories
60 kg	114 Calories	248 Calories	38 Calories

Bar Graphs

To compare how many Calories a person burns doing various activities, you could create a bar graph. A bar graph is used to display data in a number of separate, or distinct, categories. In this example, bicycling, playing basketball, and watching television are three separate categories.

To create a bar graph, follow these steps.

1. On graph paper, draw a horizontal, or *x*-, axis and a vertical, or *y*-, axis.
2. Write the names of the categories to be graphed along the horizontal axis. Include an overall label for the axis as well.
3. Label the vertical axis with the name of the responding variable. Include units of measurement. Then create a scale along the axis by marking off equally spaced numbers that cover the range of the data collected.
4. For each category, draw a solid bar using the scale on the vertical axis to determine the

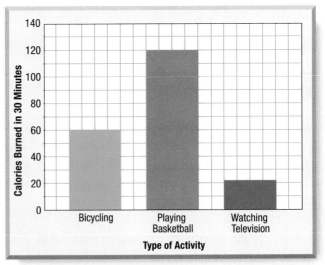

Calories Burned by a 30-kilogram Person in Various Activities

appropriate height. For example, for bicycling, draw the bar as high as the 60 mark on the vertical axis. Make all the bars the same width and leave equal spaces between them.

5. Add a title that describes the graph.

Line Graphs

To see whether a relationship exists between body mass and the number of Calories burned while bicycling, you could create a line graph. A line graph is used to display data that show how one variable (the responding variable) changes in response to another variable (the manipulated variable). You can use a line graph when your manipulated variable is *continuous*, that is, when there are other points between the ones that you tested. In this example, body mass is a continuous variable because there are other body masses between 30 and 40 kilograms (for example, 31 kilograms). Time is another example of a continuous variable.

Line graphs are powerful tools because they allow you to estimate values for conditions that you did not test in the experiment. For example, you can use the line graph to estimate that a 35-kilogram person would burn 68 Calories while bicycling.

To create a line graph, follow these steps.
1. On graph paper, draw a horizontal, or *x*-, axis and a vertical, or *y*-, axis.
2. Label the horizontal axis with the name of the manipulated variable. Label the vertical axis with the name of the responding variable. Include units of measurement.
3. Create a scale on each axis by marking off equally spaced numbers that cover the range of the data collected.
4. Plot a point on the graph for each piece of data. In the line graph above, the dotted lines show how to plot the first data point (30 kilograms and 60 Calories). Draw an imaginary vertical line extending up from the horizontal axis at the 30-kilogram mark. Then draw an imaginary horizontal line extending across from the vertical axis at the 60-Calorie mark. Plot the point where the two lines intersect.

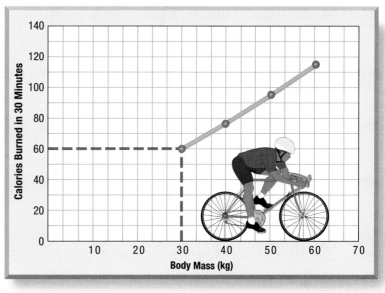

Effect of Body Mass on Calories Burned While Bicycling

5. Connect the plotted points with a solid line. (In some cases, it may be more appropriate to draw a line that shows the general trend of the plotted points. In those cases, some of the points may fall above or below the line.)
6. Add a title that identifies the variables or relationship in the graph.

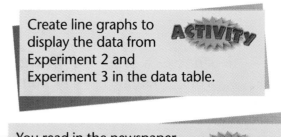

Create line graphs to display the data from Experiment 2 and Experiment 3 in the data table. **ACTIVITY**

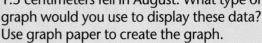

You read in the newspaper that a total of 4 centimeters of rain fell in your area in June, 2.5 centimeters fell in July, and 1.5 centimeters fell in August. What type of graph would you use to display these data? Use graph paper to create the graph. **ACTIVITY**

Circle Graphs

Like bar graphs, circle graphs can be used to display data in a number of separate categories. Unlike bar graphs, however, circle graphs can only be used when you have data for *all* the categories that make up a given topic. A circle graph is sometimes called a pie chart because it resembles a pie cut into slices. The pie represents the entire topic, while the slices represent the individual categories. The size of a slice indicates what percentage of the whole a particular category makes up.

The data table below shows the results of a survey in which 24 teenagers were asked to identify their favorite sport. The data were then used to create the circle graph at the right.

Sports That Teens Prefer

Swimming 16.7%

Soccer 33.3%

60°

120°

Bicycling 25%

90°

90°

Basketball 25%

FAVORITE SPORTS

Sport	Number of Students
Soccer	8
Basketball	6
Bicycling	6
Swimming	4

To create a circle graph, follow these steps.

1. Use a compass to draw a circle. Mark the center of the circle with a point. Then draw a line from the center point to the top of the circle.

2. Determine the size of each "slice" by setting up a proportion where *x* equals the number of degrees in a slice. (NOTE: A circle contains 360 degrees.) For example, to find the number of degrees in the "soccer" slice, set up the following proportion:

$$\frac{\text{students who prefer soccer}}{\text{total number of students}} = \frac{x}{\text{total number of degrees in a circle}}$$

$$\frac{8}{24} = \frac{x}{360}$$

Cross-multiply and solve for *x*.

$$24x = 8 \times 360$$
$$x = 120$$

The "soccer" slice should contain 120 degrees.

3. Use a protractor to measure the angle of the first slice, using the line you drew to the top of the circle as the 0° line. Draw a line from the center of the circle to the edge for the angle you measured.

4. Continue around the circle by measuring the size of each slice with the protractor. Start measuring from the edge of the previous slice so the wedges do not overlap. When you are done, the entire circle should be filled in.

5. Determine the percentage of the whole circle that each slice represents. To do this, divide the number of degrees in a slice by the total number of degrees in a circle (360), and multiply by 100%. For the "soccer" slice, you can find the percentage as follows:

$$\frac{120}{360} \times 100\% = 33.3\%$$

6. Use a different color to shade in each slice. Label each slice with the name of the category and with the percentage of the whole it represents.

7. Add a title to the circle graph.

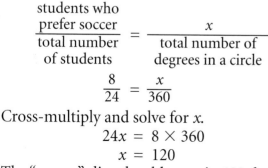

ACTIVITY

In a class of 28 students, 12 students take the bus to school, 10 students walk, and 6 students ride their bicycles. Create a circle graph to display these data.

Laboratory Safety

Safety Symbols

These symbols alert you to possible dangers in the laboratory and remind you to work carefully.

 Safety Goggles Always wear safety goggles to protect your eyes in any activity involving chemicals, flames or heating, or the possibility of broken glassware.

Lab Apron Wear a laboratory apron to protect your skin and clothing from damage.

 Breakage You are working with materials that may be breakable, such as glass containers, glass tubing, thermometers, or funnels. Handle breakable materials with care. Do not touch broken glassware.

Heat-resistant Gloves Use an oven mitt or other hand protection when handling hot materials. Hot plates, hot glassware, or hot water can cause burns. Do not touch hot objects with your bare hands.

Heating Use a clamp or tongs to pick up hot glassware. Do not touch hot objects with your bare hands.

Sharp Object Pointed-tip scissors, scalpels, knives, needles, pins, or tacks are sharp. They can cut or puncture your skin. Always direct a sharp edge or point away from yourself and others. Use sharp instruments only as instructed.

 Electric Shock Avoid the possibility of electric shock. Never use electrical equipment around water, or when the equipment is wet or your hands are wet. Be sure cords are untangled and cannot trip anyone. Disconnect the equipment when it is not in use.

Corrosive Chemical You are working with an acid or another corrosive chemical. Avoid getting it on your skin or clothing, or in your eyes. Do not inhale the vapors. Wash your hands when you are finished with the activity.

Poison Do not let any poisonous chemical come in contact with your skin, and do not inhale its vapors. Wash your hands when you are finished with the activity.

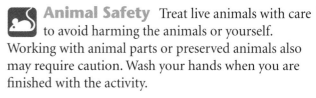 **Physical Safety** When an experiment involves physical activity, take precautions to avoid injuring yourself or others. Follow instructions from your teacher. Alert your teacher if there is any reason you should not participate in the activity.

Animal Safety Treat live animals with care to avoid harming the animals or yourself. Working with animal parts or preserved animals also may require caution. Wash your hands when you are finished with the activity.

Plant Safety Handle plants in the laboratory or during field work only as directed by your teacher. If you are allergic to certain plants, tell your teacher before doing an activity in which those plants are used. Avoid touching harmful plants such as poison ivy, poison oak, or poison sumac, or plants with thorns. Wash your hands when you are finished with the activity.

Flames You may be working with flames from a lab burner, candle, or matches. Tie back loose hair and clothing. Follow instructions from your teacher about lighting and extinguishing flames.

No Flames Flammable materials may be present. Make sure there are no flames, sparks, or other exposed heat sources present.

Fumes When poisonous or unpleasant vapors may be involved, work in a ventilated area. Avoid inhaling vapors directly. Only test an odor when directed to do so by your teacher, and use a wafting motion to direct the vapor toward your nose.

Disposal Chemicals and other laboratory materials used in the activity must be disposed of safely. Follow the instructions from your teacher.

Hand Washing Wash your hands thoroughly when finished with the activity. Use antibacterial soap and warm water. Lather both sides of your hands and between your fingers. Rinse well.

General Safety Awareness You may see this symbol when none of the symbols described earlier appears. In this case, follow the specific instructions provided. You may also see this symbol when you are asked to develop your own procedure in a lab. Have your teacher approve your plan before you go further.

Science Safety Rules

To prepare yourself to work safely in the laboratory, read over the following safety rules. Then read them a second time. Make sure you understand and follow each rule. Ask your teacher to explain any rules you do not understand.

Dress Code

1. To protect yourself from injuring your eyes, wear safety goggles whenever you work with chemicals, burners, glassware, or any substance that might get into your eyes. If you wear contact lenses, notify your teacher.
2. Wear a lab apron or coat whenever you work with corrosive chemicals or substances that can stain.
3. Tie back long hair to keep it away from any chemicals, flames, or equipment.
4. Remove or tie back any article of clothing or jewelry that can hang down and touch chemicals, flames, or equipment. Roll up or secure long sleeves.
5. Never wear open shoes or sandals.

General Precautions

6. Read all directions for an experiment several times before beginning the activity. Carefully follow all written and oral instructions. If you are in doubt about any part of the experiment, ask your teacher for assistance.
7. Never perform activities that are not assigned or authorized by your teacher. Obtain permission before "experimenting" on your own. Never handle any equipment unless you have specific permission.
8. Never perform lab activities without direct supervision.
9. Never eat or drink in the laboratory.
10. Keep work areas clean and tidy at all times. Bring only notebooks and lab manuals or written lab procedures to the work area. All other items, such as purses and backpacks, should be left in a designated area.
11. Do not engage in horseplay.

First Aid

12. Always report all accidents or injuries to your teacher, no matter how minor. Notify your teacher immediately about any fires.
13. Learn what to do in case of specific accidents, such as getting acid in your eyes or on your skin. (Rinse acids from your body with lots of water.)
14. Be aware of the location of the first-aid kit, but do not use it unless instructed by your teacher. In case of injury, your teacher should administer first aid. Your teacher may also send you to the school nurse or call a physician.
15. Know the location of emergency equipment, such as the fire extinguisher and fire blanket, and know how to use it.
16. Know the location of the nearest telephone and whom to contact in an emergency.

Heating and Fire Safety

17. Never use a heat source, such as a candle, burner, or hot plate, without wearing safety goggles.
18. Never heat anything unless instructed to do so. A chemical that is harmless when cool may be dangerous when heated.
19. Keep all combustible materials away from flames. Never use a flame or spark near a combustible chemical.
20. Never reach across a flame.
21. Before using a laboratory burner, make sure you know proper procedures for lighting and adjusting the burner, as demonstrated by your teacher. Do not touch the burner. It may be hot. And never leave a lighted burner unattended!
22. Chemicals can splash or boil out of a heated test tube. When heating a substance in a test tube, make sure that the mouth of the tube is not pointed at you or anyone else.
23. Never heat a liquid in a closed container. The expanding gases produced may blow the container apart.
24. Before picking up a container that has been heated, hold the back of your hand near it. If you can feel heat on the back of your hand, the container is too hot to handle. Use an oven mitt to pick up a container that has been heated.

Using Chemicals Safely

25. Never mix chemicals "for the fun of it." You might produce a dangerous, possibly explosive substance.

26. Never put your face near the mouth of a container that holds chemicals. Never touch, taste, or smell a chemical unless you are instructed by your teacher to do so. Many chemicals are poisonous.

27. Use only those chemicals needed in the activity. Read and double-check labels on supply bottles before removing any chemicals. Take only as much as you need. Keep all containers closed when chemicals are not being used.

28. Dispose of all chemicals as instructed by your teacher. To avoid contamination, never return chemicals to their original containers. Never simply pour chemicals or other substances into the sink or trash containers.

29. Be extra careful when working with acids or bases. Pour all chemicals over the sink or a container, not over your work surface.

30. If you are instructed to test for odors, use a wafting motion to direct the odors to your nose. Do not inhale the fumes directly from the container.

31. When mixing an acid and water, always pour the water into the container first and then add the acid to the water. Never pour water into an acid.

32. Take extreme care not to spill any material in the laboratory. Wash chemical spills and splashes immediately with plenty of water. Immediately begin rinsing with water any acids that get on your skin or clothing, and notify your teacher of any acid spill at the same time.

Using Glassware Safely

33. Never force glass tubing or thermometers into a rubber stopper or rubber tubing. Have your teacher insert the glass tubing or thermometer if required for an activity.

34. If you are using a laboratory burner, use a wire screen to protect glassware from any flame. Never heat glassware that is not thoroughly dry on the outside.

35. Keep in mind that hot glassware looks cool. Never pick up glassware without first checking to see if it is hot. Use an oven mitt. See rule 24.

36. Never use broken or chipped glassware. If glassware breaks, notify your teacher and dispose of the glassware in the proper broken-glassware container. Never handle broken glass with your bare hands.

37. Never eat or drink from lab glassware.

38. Thoroughly clean glassware before putting it away.

Using Sharp Instruments

39. Handle scalpels or other sharp instruments with extreme care. Never cut material toward you; cut away from you.

40. Immediately notify your teacher if you cut your skin when working in the laboratory.

Animal and Plant Safety

41. Never perform experiments that cause pain, discomfort, or harm to mammals, birds, reptiles, fishes, or amphibians. This rule applies at home as well as in the classroom.

42. Animals should be handled only if absolutely necessary. Your teacher will instruct you as to how to handle each animal species brought into the classroom.

43. If you know that you are allergic to certain plants, molds, or animals, tell your teacher before doing an activity in which these are used.

44. During field work, protect your skin by wearing long pants, long sleeves, socks, and closed shoes. Know how to recognize the poisonous plants and fungi in your area, as well as plants with thorns, and avoid contact with them.

45. Never eat any part of an unidentified plant or fungus.

46. Wash your hands thoroughly after handling animals or the cage containing animals. Wash your hands when you are finished with any activity involving animal parts, plants, or soil.

End-of-Experiment Rules

47. After an experiment has been completed, clean up your work area and return all equipment to its proper place.

48. Dispose of waste materials as instructed by your teacher.

49. Wash your hands after every experiment.

50. Always turn off all burners or hot plates when they are not in use. Unplug hot plates and other electrical equipment. If you used a burner, check that the gas-line valve to the burner is off as well.

Using a Laboratory Balance

The laboratory balance is an important tool in scientific investigations. You can use a balance to determine the masses of materials that you study or experiment with in the laboratory.

Different kinds of balances are used in the laboratory. One kind of balance is the triple-beam balance. The balance that you may use in your science class is probably similar to the balance illustrated in this Appendix. To use the balance properly, you should learn the name, location, and function of each part of the balance you are using. What kind of balance do you have in your science class?

The Triple-Beam Balance

The triple-beam balance is a single-pan balance with three beams calibrated in grams. The back, or 100-gram, beam is divided into ten units of 10 grams each. The middle, or 500-gram, beam is divided into five units of 100 grams each. The front, or 10-gram, beam is divided into ten major units of 1 gram each. Each of these units is further divided into units of 0.1 gram. What is the largest mass you could find with a triple-beam balance?

The following procedure can be used to find the mass of an object with a triple-beam balance:

1. Place the object on the pan.
2. Move the rider on the middle beam notch by notch until the horizontal pointer drops below zero. Move the rider back one notch.
3. Move the rider on the back beam notch by notch until the pointer again drops below zero. Move the rider back one notch.
4. Slowly slide the rider along the front beam until the pointer stops at the zero point.
5. The mass of the object is equal to the sum of the readings on the three beams.

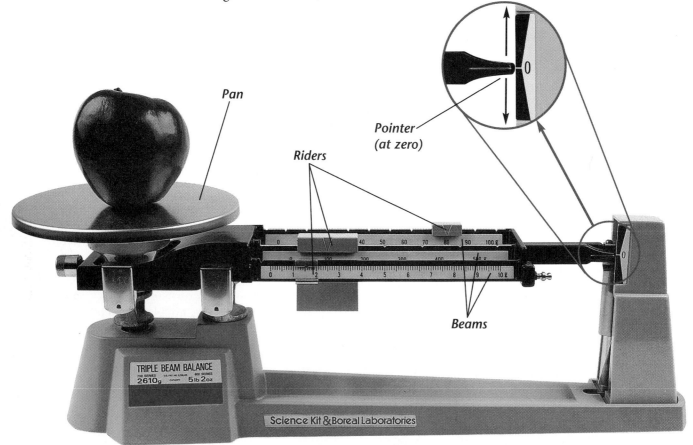

Triple-Beam Balance

List of Chemical Elements

Name	Symbol	Atomic Number	Atomic Mass†
Actinium	Ac	89	227.028
Aluminum	Al	13	26.982
Americium	Am	95	(243)
Antimony	Sb	51	121.75
Argon	Ar	18	39.948
Arsenic	As	33	74.922
Astatine	At	85	(210)
Barium	Ba	56	137.327
Berkelium	Bk	97	(247)
Beryllium	Be	4	9.012
Bismuth	Bi	83	208.980
Bohrium	Bh	107	(262)
Boron	B	5	10.811
Bromine	Br	35	79.904
Cadmium	Cd	48	112.411
Calcium	Ca	20	40.078
Californium	Cf	98	(251)
Carbon	C	6	12.011
Cerium	Ce	58	140.115
Cesium	Cs	55	132.905
Chlorine	Cl	17	35.453
Chromium	Cr	24	51.996
Cobalt	Co	27	58.933
Copper	Cu	29	63.546
Curium	Cm	96	(247)
Dubnium	Db	105	(262)
Dysprosium	Dy	66	162.50
Einsteinium	Es	99	(252)
Erbium	Er	68	167.26
Europium	Eu	63	151.965
Fermium	Fm	100	(257)
Fluorine	F	9	18.998
Francium	Fr	87	(223)
Gadolinium	Gd	64	157.25
Gallium	Ga	31	69.723
Germanium	Ge	32	72.61
Gold	Au	79	196.967
Hafnium	Hf	72	178.49
Hassium	Hs	108	(265)
Helium	He	2	4.003
Holmium	Ho	67	164.930
Hydrogen	H	1	1.008
Indium	In	49	114.818
Iodine	I	53	126.904
Iridium	Ir	77	192.22
Iron	Fe	26	55.847
Krypton	Kr	36	83.80
Lanthanum	La	57	138.906
Lawrencium	Lr	103	(260)
Lead	Pb	82	207.2
Lithium	Li	3	6.941
Lutetium	Lu	71	174.967
Magnesium	Mg	12	24.305
Manganese	Mn	25	54.938
Meitnerium	Mt	109	(266)
Mendelevium	Md	101	(258)

Name	Symbol	Atomic Number	Atomic Mass†
Mercury	Hg	80	200.659
Molybdenum	Mo	42	95.94
Neodymium	Nd	60	144.2
Neon	Ne	10	20.180
Neptunium	Np	93	237.048
Nickel	Ni	28	58.69
Niobium	Nb	41	92.906
Nitrogen	N	7	14.007
Nobelium	No	102	(259)
Osmium	Os	76	190.23
Oxygen	O	8	15.999
Palladium	Pd	46	106.42
Phosphorus	P	15	30.974
Platinum	Pt	78	195.08
Plutonium	Pu	94	(244)
Polonium	Po	84	(209)
Potassium	K	19	39.098
Praseodymium	Pr	59	140.908
Promethium	Pm	61	(145)
Protactinium	Pa	91	231.036
Radium	Ra	88	226.025
Radon	Rn	86	(222)
Rhenium	Re	75	186.207
Rhodium	Rh	45	102.906
Rubidium	Rb	37	85.468
Ruthenium	Ru	44	101.07
Rutherfordium	Rf	104	(261)
Samarium	Sm	62	150.36
Scandium	Sc	21	44.956
Seaborgium	Sg	106	(263)
Selenium	Se	34	78.96
Silicon	Si	14	28.086
Silver	Ag	47	107.868
Sodium	Na	11	22.990
Strontium	Sr	38	87.62
Sulfur	S	16	32.066
Tantalum	Ta	73	180.948
Technetium	Tc	43	(98)
Tellurium	Te	52	127.60
Terbium	Tb	65	158.925
Thallium	Tl	81	204.383
Thorium	Th	90	232.038
Thulium	Tm	69	168.934
Tin	Sn	50	118.710
Titanium	Ti	22	47.88
Tungsten	W	74	183.85
Ununnilium	Uun	110	(269)
Unununium	Uuu	111	(272)
Ununbium	Uub	112	(272)
Uranium	U	92	238.029
Vanadium	V	23	50.942
Xenon	Xe	54	131.29
Ytterbium	Yb	70	173.04
Yttrium	Y	39	88.906
Zinc	Zn	30	65.39
Zirconium	Zr	40	91.224

†Numbers in parentheses give the mass number of the most stable isotope.

Periodic Table of the Elements

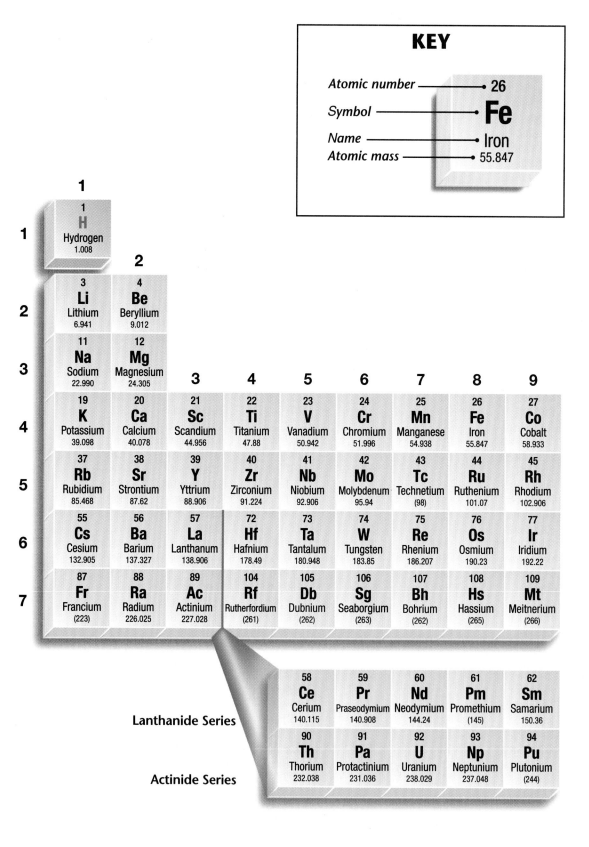

KEY

Atomic number —— 26
Symbol —— **Fe**
Name —— Iron
Atomic mass —— 55.847

1								
1 1 **H** Hydrogen 1.008								

| | 2 | | 3 | 4 | 5 | 6 | 7 | 8 | 9 |

2	3 **Li** Lithium 6.941	4 **Be** Beryllium 9.012							
3	11 **Na** Sodium 22.990	12 **Mg** Magnesium 24.305							
4	19 **K** Potassium 39.098	20 **Ca** Calcium 40.078	21 **Sc** Scandium 44.956	22 **Ti** Titanium 47.88	23 **V** Vanadium 50.942	24 **Cr** Chromium 51.996	25 **Mn** Manganese 54.938	26 **Fe** Iron 55.847	27 **Co** Cobalt 58.933
5	37 **Rb** Rubidium 85.468	38 **Sr** Strontium 87.62	39 **Y** Yttrium 88.906	40 **Zr** Zirconium 91.224	41 **Nb** Niobium 92.906	42 **Mo** Molybdenum 95.94	43 **Tc** Technetium (98)	44 **Ru** Ruthenium 101.07	45 **Rh** Rhodium 102.906
6	55 **Cs** Cesium 132.905	56 **Ba** Barium 137.327	57 **La** Lanthanum 138.906	72 **Hf** Hafnium 178.49	73 **Ta** Tantalum 180.948	74 **W** Tungsten 183.85	75 **Re** Rhenium 186.207	76 **Os** Osmium 190.23	77 **Ir** Iridium 192.22
7	87 **Fr** Francium (223)	88 **Ra** Radium 226.025	89 **Ac** Actinium 227.028	104 **Rf** Rutherfordium (261)	105 **Db** Dubnium (262)	106 **Sg** Seaborgium (263)	107 **Bh** Bohrium (262)	108 **Hs** Hassium (265)	109 **Mt** Meitnerium (266)

Lanthanide Series

58 **Ce** Cerium 140.115	59 **Pr** Praseodymium 140.908	60 **Nd** Neodymium 144.24	61 **Pm** Promethium (145)	62 **Sm** Samarium 150.36
90 **Th** Thorium 232.038	91 **Pa** Protactinium 231.036	92 **U** Uranium 238.029	93 **Np** Neptunium 237.048	94 **Pu** Plutonium (244)

Actinide Series

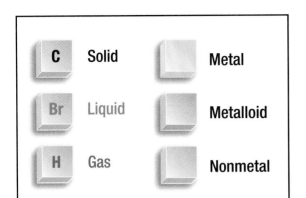

							18
							2 **He** Helium 4.003

			13	14	15	16	17	
			5 **B** Boron 10.811	6 **C** Carbon 12.011	7 **N** Nitrogen 14.007	8 **O** Oxygen 15.999	9 **F** Fluorine 18.998	10 **Ne** Neon 20.180
			13 **Al** Aluminum 26.982	14 **Si** Silicon 28.086	15 **P** Phosphorus 30.974	16 **S** Sulfur 32.066	17 **Cl** Chlorine 35.453	18 **Ar** Argon 39.948

10	11	12						
28 **Ni** Nickel 58.69	29 **Cu** Copper 63.546	30 **Zn** Zinc 65.39	31 **Ga** Gallium 69.723	32 **Ge** Germanium 72.61	33 **As** Arsenic 74.922	34 **Se** Selenium 78.96	35 **Br** Bromine 79.904	36 **Kr** Krypton 83.80
46 **Pd** Palladium 106.42	47 **Ag** Silver 107.868	48 **Cd** Cadmium 112.411	49 **In** Indium 114.818	50 **Sn** Tin 118.710	51 **Sb** Antimony 121.75	52 **Te** Tellurium 127.60	53 **I** Iodine 126.904	54 **Xe** Xenon 131.29
78 **Pt** Platinum 195.08	79 **Au** Gold 196.967	80 **Hg** Mercury 200.59	81 **Tl** Thallium 204.383	82 **Pb** Lead 207.2	83 **Bi** Bismuth 208.980	84 **Po** Polonium (209)	85 **At** Astatine (210)	86 **Rn** Radon (222)
110 **Uun** Ununnilium (269)	111 **Uuu** Unununium (272)	112 **Uub** Ununbium (272)						

The symbols shown for elements 110-112 are being used temporarily until names for these elements can be agreed upon.

63 **Eu** Europium 151.965	64 **Gd** Gadolinium 157.25	65 **Tb** Terbium 158.925	66 **Dy** Dysprosium 162.50	67 **Ho** Holmium 164.930	68 **Er** Erbium 167.26	69 **Tm** Thulium 168.934	70 **Yb** Ytterbium 173.04	71 **Lu** Lutetium 174.967
95 **Am** Americium (243)	96 **Cm** Curium (247)	97 **Bk** Berkelium (247)	98 **Cf** Californium (251)	99 **Es** Einsteinium (252)	100 **Fm** Fermium (257)	101 **Md** Mendelevium (258)	102 **No** Nobelium (259)	103 **Lr** Lawrencium (260)

Mass numbers in parentheses are those of the most stable or common isotope.

A

actinide An element in the second row of the rare earth elements in the periodic table. (p. 92)

alcohol A substituted hydrocarbon that contains one or more hydroxyl groups. (p. 122)

alkali metal An element in Group 1 of the periodic table. (p. 89)

alkaline earth metal An element in Group 2 of the periodic table. (p. 90)

alloy A mixture of two or more metals. (p. 89)

amino acid One of 20 kinds of organic compounds that are the monomers of proteins. (p. 129)

amorphous solid A solid made up of particles that are not arranged in a regular pattern. (p. 46)

atom The smallest particle of an element. (p. 30)

atomic mass The average mass of one atom of an element. (p. 77)

atomic mass unit (amu) A unit used to measure the mass of particles in atoms; a proton or neutron has a mass of 1 amu. (p. 79)

atomic number The number of protons in the nucleus of an atom. (p. 79)

B

boiling The process that occurs when vaporization takes place inside a liquid as well as on the surface. (p. 65)

boiling point The temperature at which a substance changes from a liquid to a gas. (p. 16)

Boyle's law The relationship between the pressure and volume of a gas; when volume increases, pressure decreases. (p. 52)

C

carbohydrate An energy-rich organic compound made of the elements carbon, hydrogen, and oxygen. (p. 126)

carboxyl group A –COOH group, found in organic acids. (p. 123)

cellulose A complex carbohydrate found in plant structures. (p. 128)

characteristic property A quality of a substance that never changes and can be used to identify the substance (p. 15)

Charles's law The relationship between the temperature and volume of a gas; when temperature increases, volume increases. (p. 54)

chemical activity A characteristic property of a substance that indicates its ability to undergo a specific chemical change. (p. 17)

chemical bond The force that holds two atoms together. (p. 32)

chemical change A change in which one or more substances combine or break apart to form new substances. (p. 17)

chemical energy A form of energy that comes from chemical bonds. (p. 63)

chemical reaction A process in which substances undergo chemical changes, forming new substances with different properties. (p. 68)

chemical symbol A one- or two-letter representation of an element. (p. 82)

cholesterol A waxy lipid found in all animal cells. (p. 130)

complex carbohydrate A long chain, or polymer, of simple carbohydrates. (p. 127)

compound A substance made of two or more elements chemically combined. (p. 21)

condensation The change of state from a gas to a liquid. (p. 66)

conductor A substance that transmits heat or electricity easily. (p. 88)

controlled experiment An experiment in which all factors except one are kept constant. (p. 153)

corrosion The gradual wearing away of a metal element due to a chemical reaction. (p. 88)

crystalline solid A substance that is made up of crystals in which particles are arranged in a regular, repeating pattern. (p. 46)

D

density The measurement of how much mass of a substance is contained in a given volume. (p. 26)

diamond A form of the element carbon; it is the hardest mineral crystal on Earth. (p. 114)

diatomic molecule A molecule composed of two atoms. (p. 97)

digestion The process of breaking polymers into monomers by means of a chemical change. (p. 126)

directly proportional A term used to describe the relationship between two variables whose graph is a straight line passing through the point (0, 0). (p. 58)

DNA *DeoxyriboNucleic Acid.* (p. 132)

ductile A term used to describe a material that can be pulled out into a long wire. (p. 87)

electrode A metal strip used in electrolysis. (p. 36)

electrolysis A process by which an electric current breaks chemical bonds. (p. 36)

electron A tiny, negatively charged particle that moves around the nucleus of an atom. (p. 79)

element A substance that cannot be broken down into other substances by chemical or physical means. (p. 19)

ester An organic compound made by chemically combining an alcohol and an organic acid. (p. 123)

evaporation The process that occurs when vaporization takes place only on the surface of a liquid. (p. 65)

family Elements in the same vertical column of the periodic table; also called group. (p. 82)

fatty acid An organic compound that is a monomer of a fat or oil. (p. 130)

fluid Any substance that can flow. (p. 47)

freezing The change in state from a liquid to a solid. (p. 64)

fullerene A form of the element carbon that consists of carbon atoms arranged in a repeating pattern similar to the surface of a soccer ball. (p. 115)

gas A state of matter with no definite shape or volume. (p. 47)

glucose A sugar found in the body; the monomer of many complex carbohydrates. (p. 127)

graph A diagram that shows how two variables are related. (p. 56)

graphite A form of the element carbon in which carbon atoms form flat layers. (p. 114)

group Elements in the same vertical column of the periodic table; also called family. (p. 82)

halogen family The elements in Group 17 of the periodic table. (p. 100)

hydrocarbon An organic compound that contains only carbon and hydrogen. (p. 118)

hydroxyl group An –OH group, found in alcohols. (p. 122)

hypothesis A prediction about the outcome of an experiment. (p. 152)

International System of Units (SI) The system of units used by scientists to measure the properties of matter. (p. 23)

isomer One of a number of compounds that have the same molecular formula but different structures. (p. 120)

lanthanide An element in the first row of the rare earth elements in the periodic table. (p. 92)

law of conservation of energy The principle that the total amount of energy remains the same during physical or chemical change. (p. 63)

lipid An energy-rich polymer made of carbon, oxygen, and hydrogen; fats, oils, waxes, and cholesterol are lipids. (p. 130)

liquid A state of matter that has no definite shape but has a definite volume. (p. 46)

magnetic A characteristic of those metals that are attracted to magnets and can be made into magnets. (p. 88)

malleable A term used to describe material that can be hammered or rolled into shape. (p. 87)

manipulated variable The one factor that a scientist changes during an experiment. (p. 153)

mass A measure of how much matter is in an object. (p. 23)

melting The change in state from a solid to a liquid. (p. 64)

melting point The temperature at which a substance changes from a solid to a liquid. (p. 16)

metalloid An element that has some of the characteristics of metals and some of the characteristics of nonmetals. (p. 101)

mineral A simple element needed by the body, that is not organic. (p. 133)

mixture Two or more substances that are mixed together but not chemically combined. (p. 18)

molecular formula A combination of chemical symbols that represent the elements in each molecule of a compound. (p. 119)

molecule A combination of two or more atoms. (p. 32)

monomer One molecule that makes up the links in a polymer chain. (p. 124)

neutron A small particle in the nucleus of the atom, with no electrical charge. (p. 79)

noble gas An element in Group 18 of the periodic table. (p. 100)

nonmetal An element that lacks most of the properties of metals. (p. 96)

nuclear fusion The process in which smaller nuclei combine into larger nuclei, forming heavier elements. (p. 105)

nucleic acid A very large organic compound made up of carbon, oxygen, hydrogen, nitrogen, and phosphorus; examples are DNA and RNA. (p. 132)

nucleotide An organic compound that is one of the monomers of nucleic acids. (p. 132)

nucleus The central core of an atom containing protons and usually neutrons. (p. 79)

nutrient A substance that provides energy or raw materials for the body to grow, repair worn parts, or function properly. (p. 126)

operational definition A statement that describes how a particular variable is to be measured or a term is to be defined. (p. 153)

ore A rock that contains a metal or other economically useful element. (p. 35)

organic acid A substituted hydrocarbon with one or more of the –COOH group of atoms. (p. 123)

organic compounds Most compounds that contain carbon. (p. 117)

period A horizontal row of elements in the periodic table. (p. 83)

periodic table A chart of the elements showing the repeating pattern of their properties. (p. 78)

physical change A change in a substance that does not change its identity; for example, a change of state. (p. 17)

plasma A state of matter in which atoms are stripped of their electrons and the nuclei packed closely together. (p. 104)

polymer A large molecule in the form of a chain in which many smaller molecules are bonded together. (p. 124)

pressure The force pushing on a surface divided by the area of that surface. (p. 51)

protein An organic compound that is a polymer of amino acids. (p. 129)

proton A small, positively charged particle in the nucleus of the atom. (p. 79)

pure substance A substance made of only one kind of matter and having definite properties. (p. 19)

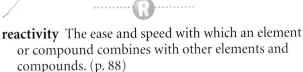

reactivity The ease and speed with which an element or compound combines with other elements and compounds. (p. 88)

responding variable The factor that changes as a result of a change to the manipulated variable in an experiment. (p. 153)

RNA *RiboNucleic Acid.* (p. 132)

saturated hydrocarbons A hydrocarbon in which all the bonds between carbon atoms are single bonds. (p. 121)

semiconductor An element that can conduct electricity under some conditions. (p. 101)

solid A state of matter that has a definite volume and a definite shape. (p. 45)

solution A very well-mixed mixture. (p. 18)

starch A complex carbohydrate in which plants store energy. (p. 128)

structural formula A description of a molecule that shows the kind, number, and arrangement of atoms. (p. 120)

sublimation The change in state from a solid directly to a gas without passing through the liquid state. (p. 66)

subscript A number in a formula written lower and smaller than the symbol to indicate the number of atoms of an element in a molecule. (p. 119)

substituted hydrocarbon A hydrocarbon in which one or more hydrogen atoms have been replaced by atoms of other elements. (p. 122)

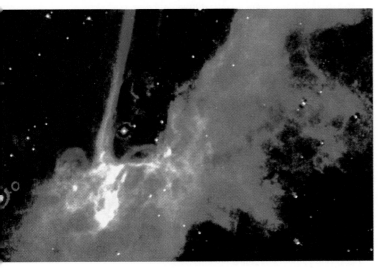

supernova An explosion of a massive star. (p. 106)

synthetic A material that is not formed naturally but is manufactured. (p. 124)

temperature A measure of the average energy of motion of the particles of a substance. (p. 50)

thermal energy The total energy of a substance's particles due to their movement or vibration. (p. 63)

transition metal An element in Groups 3 through 12 of the periodic table. (p. 90)

unsaturated hydrocarbon A hydrocarbon in which one or more of the bonds between carbon atoms is double or triple. (p. 121)

valence electron One of the electrons farthest away from the nucleus of the atom; these electrons are involved in a chemical reaction. (p. 85)

vaporization The change of state from a liquid to a gas. (p. 65)

variable Any factor that can change in an experiment. (p. 153)

vary inversely A term used to describe the relationship between two variables whose graph forms a curve that slopes downward. (p. 59)

viscosity The resistance of a liquid to flowing. (p. 47)

vitamin An organic compound that serves as a helper molecule in a variety of chemical reactions in the body. (p. 133)

volume The amount of space that matter occupies. (p. 23)

weight A measure of the force of gravity on an object. (p. 23)

Index

Acknowledgments

Illustration

Annie Bissett: 140, 141, 144, 145
Peter Brooks: 28, 36, 60, 70, 94, 102, 116, 134
Annette Cable: 10tl, 11tr
Andrea Golden: 10–11tm
Martucci Design: 57b, 58t, 59, 113tr, 158, 159, 160,
Matt Mayerchak: 40, 108, 138, 156, 157,
Morgan Cain & Associates: 23, 32, 37, 45, 46, 48, 51, 52, 53, 54, 57t, 58b, 65, 79, 80–81, 82, 83, 86, 90, 91, 92, 97, 98 99, 100, 101, 105, 106, 113tl, 113m, 113br, 114, 115, 131, 150, 151, 166–167
Ortelius Design Inc.: 24–25
J/B Woolsey Associates: 154

Photography

Photo Research by Sue McDermott
Cover image G. Tomich/Photo Researchers

Nature of Science
Page 8t, Holt Studios International/Photo Researchers; **8b,** Andy Goodwin/Discover Magazine; **9t,** Courtesy of Rathin Datta; **9b,** Martin Bond/SDL/Photo Researchers; **10,** Paul Conklin/PhotoEdit.

Chapter 1
Pages 12–13, Cameron Davidson/TSI; **14,** Russ Lappa; **15,** Tim Hauf/Visuals Unlimited; **16,** Jim Corwin/TSI; **17,** John M. Roberts/The Stock Market; **17 inset,** E.R. Degginger/Animals Animals/Earth Scenes; **18,** Richard Haynes; **19l,** Mark E. Gibson/Visuals Unlimited; **19r,** Ron Testa/The Field Museum, Chicago, IL; **20t,** David D. Keaton/The Stock Market; **20ml,** Michael Fogden/DRK Photo; **20mr,** Glenn M. Oliver/Visuals Unlimited; **20bl,** Richard Megna/Fundamental Photographs; **20bml,** Charles Gupton/TSI; **20bmr,** Goivaux Communication/Phototake; **20br,** Ken Lucas/Visuals Unlimited; **21,** Lawrence Migdale/TSI; **22t,** Richard Haynes; **22b,** Mark Thayer; **23l,** Russ Lappa; **23r,** Richard Haynes; **24t, 25t,** Corbis-Bettmann; **25b,** The Granger Collection, NY; **26,** Pal Hermansen/TSI; **29 both,** 1998, The Art Institute of Chicago; **30t,** Rich Treptow/Visuals Unlimited; **30b,** The Granger Collection, NY; **31,** Chuck Feil/Uniphoto; **32,** Professor K. Seddon, Queen's University Belfast/Science Photo Library/Photo Researchers; **33,** SCI-VU-IBMRL/Visuals Unlimited; **34t,** Russ Lappa; **34b,** Corbis-Bettmann; **35t,** Helga Lade/Peter Arnold; **35bl,** E.R. Degginger/Animals Animals/Earth Scenes; **35br,** Charles D. Winters/Photo Researchers; **36,** Aron Haupt/David R. Frazier Photo Library; **38,** Heine Schneebeli/Science Photo Library/Photo Researchers; **39l,** Corbis-Bettmann; **39r,** Helga Lade/Peter Arnold.

Chapter 2
Pages 42–43, Milton Rand/Tom Stack & Associates; **44t,** Richard Haynes; **44b,** Shambroom/Photo Researchers; **45,** Darryl Torckler/TSI; **46t,** Superstock; **46b,** Russ Lappa; **47,** Tsutomu Nakayama/Uniphoto; **48,** Tomas Muscionoco/The Stock Market; **49,** A. Ramey/Stock Boston; **50,** John D. Cunningham/Visuals Unlimited; **51, 52,** Richard Haynes; **53,** Ken Ross/FPG International; **55l,** Michelle Bridwell/PhotoEdit; **55r,** Rudi Von Briel/PhotoEdit; **60,** Russ Lappa; **61,** Richard Haynes; **62 both,** Russ Lappa; **63l,** Doug Martin/Photo Researchers; **63r,** Tony Freeman/PhotoEdit; **64,** Granger Collection, NY; **65t,** Larry Lefter/Grant Heilman Photography; **65b,** Martin Dohrn/Science Photo Library/Photo Researchers; **66t,** Richard Haynes; **66b,** Charles D. Winters/Photo Researchers; **68l,** Steve Taylor/TSI; **68r,** Dollarhide/Monkmeyer; **69,** David Young Wolff/TSI; **70,** Russ Lappa; **71,** Darryl Torckler/TSI.

Chapter 3
Pages 74–75, Roy King/Superstock; **76 both,** Russ Lappa; **77t,** Jo Prater/Visuals Unlimited; **77 inset,** Peter L. Chapman/Stock Boston; **77b,** Russ Lappa; **78 both,** The Granger Collection, NY; **83,** Russ Lappa; **84t,** The Granger Collection, NY; **84b,** Cecile Brunswick/Peter Arnold; **85t,** Alexander Tsiaras/Stock Boston; **85b,** AIP Emilio Segre Visual Archives; **87,** Nubar Alexanian/Stock Boston; **88tl,** Russ Lappa; **88tr,** Stephen Frisch/Stock Boston; **88m,** Russ Lappa; **88b,** Charles D. Winters/Photo Researchers; **89,** Jeremy Scott/International Stock; **90l,** Claire Paxton & Jacqui Farrow/Science Photo Library/ Photo Researchers; **90r,** David Noton/International Stock; **91,** Russ Lappa; **92,** Steve Wanke/Uniphoto; **93,** Bob Daemmrich/Stock Boston; **94,** Russ Lappa; **95 both,** Richard Haynes; **96,** Tom Brakefield/The Stock Market; **97,** Lawrence Migdale/Science Source/Photo Researchers; **98l,** Charles D. Winters/Photo Researchers; **98r,** Mark Gibson/Visuals Unlimited; **99,** Novovitch/Liaison International; **100t,** Michael Dalton/Fundamental Photographs; **100b,** Stephen Frisch/Stock Boston; **101,** Roger Du Buisson/The Stock Market; **103,** Francois Gohier/Photo Researchers; **104,** David Nunuk/Science Photo Library/Photo Researchers; **105,** NASA; **106,** Space Telescope Science Institute; **107,** Novovitch/Liaison International.

Chapter 4
Pages 110–111, James Schnepf/Liaison International; **112,** Vision Agenzia Fotografica/Photo Researchers, Inc.; **114t,** Martin Rogers/TSI; **114b,** Russ Lappa; **115t,** Richard Pasley/Stock Boston; **115b, 116,** Russ Lappa; **117t,** Richard Haynes; **117b,** Bob Daemmrich/Stock Boston; **118l,** Frank Oberle/TSI; **118m,** William Taufic/The Stock Market; **118r,** Jeffery Mark Dunn/The Stock Market; **119,** Matthew Naythons/The Stock Market; **120,** David J. Sams/Stock Boston; **121l,** Russ Lappa; **121r,** Novosti/Photo Researchers; **122,** John Edwards/TSI; **123t,** R.J. Erwin/Photo Researchers; **123b, 124l,** Russ Lappa; **124r,** Daniel McDonald/Stock Boston; **125t,** Russ Lappa; **125b,** Kenneth Chen/Envision; **126,** Tony Freeman/PhotoEdit; **127, 128 both, 129, 130tl,tr,** Russ Lappa; **130b,** Cabisco/Visuals Unlimited; **132l,** Joe McDonald/Visuals Unlimited; **132r,** David Parker/Science Photo Library/Photo Researchers; **133, 134,** Russ Lappa; **135,** Richard Haynes; **136,** Mike Mazzaschi/Stock Boston; **137t,** Richard Pasley/Stock Boston; **137r,** David Parker/Science Photo Library/Photo Researchers.

Interdisciplinary Exploration
Page 144t, Peter Johansky/Envision; **144b,** Lawrence Migdale/TSI; **145t,** Russ Lappa; **145m,** Bill Aron/TSI; **145b,** Steven Needham/Envision; **146t,** Tony Freeman/Photo Edit; **146–147,** Paul Chesley/TSI; **147t,** Russ Lappa.

Skills Handbook
Page 148, Mike Moreland/Photo Network; **149t,** Foodpix; **149m,** Richard Haynes; **149b,** Russ Lappa; **152,** Richard Haynes; **154,** Ron Kimball; **155,** Renee Lynn/Photo Researchers.